These Potatoes Look Like Humans

These Potatoes Look Like Humans

The Contested Future of the Land,
Home and Death in South Africa

uMbuso weNkosi

WITS UNIVERSITY PRESS

Published in South Africa by:
Wits University Press
1 Jan Smuts Avenue
Johannesburg 2001

www.witspress.co.za

First published 2023

http://dx.doi.org.10.18772/12023098400

978-1-77614-840-0 (Paperback)
978-1-77614-841-7 (Hardback)
978-1-77614-842-4 (Web PDF)
978-1-77614-843-1 (EPUB)

This publication is peer reviewed following international best practice standards for academic and scholarly books.

Project manager: Lisa Compton
Copyeditor: Alison Lowry
Proofreader: Inga Norenius
Indexer: Sanet le Roux
Cover design: Hybrid Creative
Typeset in 11.5 point Crimson

In loving memory of Mpho Mulalo Ratshilumela
(28 November 2014 – 7 December 2021)
&
Thoko Nellie Nkosi
(26 February 1954 – 24 September 2022)

Contents

List of illustrations   ix

Acknowledgements   xi

Prologue: Emazambaneni: The land of terror   1

1   The spectre of the human potato   11

2   Whose eyes are looking at history?   31

3   Bethal, the house of God   51

4   Violence: The white farmers' fears erupt   77

5   These eyes are looking for a home   97

6   Bethal today   115

7   Our eschatological future   131

    Notes   141

    Bibliography   157

    Index   165

Illustrations

Figure 0.1 Prisoner's letter smuggled from Leslie jail, 1954   2–3

Figure 1.1 Farmworkers working the fields in Bethal, 1952   14

Figure 1.2 ANC activists, wearing potato sacks, carry a coffin at
a funeral, 1959   16

Figure 3.1 Ruins of a church in Bethal, 1901   53

Figure 3.2 Boss-boy on horseback monitoring farmworkers, 1952   56

Figure 3.3 Child labour on a Bethal farm, 1952   64

Figure 3.4 Bethal farmworkers – mostly children – being
monitored by a boss-boy, 1952   67

Figure 6.1 Map showing farms visited in the Bethal area   117

Acknowledgements

In every book lies the hidden biography of the author. The book, however, stands on its own. The biography remains concealed. It gets revealed only when we look at the narrative voice of the author – the desire of the author to understand themselves and the world they inhabit.

This book was set for me before I even started. Storytelling comes from my mother, who used to tell me stories of Shakespearean tragedies, especially that of Julius Caesar. She told me about the power of Shakespeare and how his view of life influenced the reading of history and world events. Within a Shakespearean tragedy lie contradictions that look easily solvable, yet once you engage the contradictions, the solution is not so simple. Every author aims to construct that puzzle in a book and then conceal themselves. The reader finds what will speak to them. I was never a happy child, because I realised that the world is so evil because it has so many people who claim to be good. My mother was the one who told me that to deal with tragedy one must have patience – and the patience I have is inherited from my father, Mzikayifane Brian Dongo. This book as it stands today is a product of forces that go beyond my own biography, revealing a desire to speak far beyond this present and into the future. So, I am grateful for that spirit.

This book is only the beginning, revealing a certain consciousness at a certain time of my life. Many more books will come, even if not written by me.

I must extend my gratitude to many. To my family for letting me be. Nokuphiwe, the first friend and cheerleader I had in the family. To my uncles, Linda, Mgcina and Lungi, who were fathers to me. To Malume Funky, Dumi, Jabu, Mandla, Bozo, Sipho, Thogwane, Chikwane, Sifiso, Bodloza and Nhlanhla. Chikwane, thank you for the hyena and the enormous energy; it fills my study. My young mother Ntombikayise Currien Nkosi (Sis Ntonto), mrangci, the one who believes that tomorrow I can change the world. Siyabonga, my son, who I hope will shape his own future and do it like the great individual he is. Owami and Owethu (my twins), I hope to see you grow to become responsible men in society. Buhle (my beautiful angel), as you would say, 'ngikuthanda ngenhliziyo yami yonke'. To my nieces and nephews, Mbali, Nonhle, Nkosingiphile and Lethokuhle – thank you for always making me laugh, even when I had no reason to. My challenge remains to continue following in the great footsteps of all members of my family and to lead by example for those who come after me. Then there is Chancellor Tomti 'Makhandakhanda' 'Dlamini'. Thank you for your companionship during those times when I was very lonely! Book Professor 'Zam Zam', thanks for making me laugh.

To my late grandmother Mary Sithandwa Nkosi, thanks for instilling humility and accountability in me at an early age. My late grandfather Aaron Nkosi, the wise one, is my example of taking responsibility in life. I remember the day I walked into the Johannesburg Institute for Advanced Study (JIAS) offices to meet Bongani Ngqulunga to discuss the possibility of pursuing a postdoctoral fellowship. That day I saw the spirit of Oliver Reginald Tambo as I confabulated with you, Ngqulunga, Majola, Magcingwane. Thank you for your support. My colleagues at JIAS, Daniella Rafaely, Prinola Govenden, Moorosi Leshoele, David Wa Maahlamela, Vidette Bester, Joseph Makanda – thank you for the encouragement while I was working on the manuscript.

The book stems from an award I received for my PhD thesis. The award, by the Faculty of Humanities' PhD to Monograph Initiative at the University of the Witwatersrand, Johannesburg, recognises excellent doctoral work and provides for the conversion of the thesis into the publication of a book to establish emerging academics.

I received feedback on my writing from Brenda Cooper and editorial support from Monica Seeber, who passed away and did not see the final product (may her soul rest in peace). Alison Lowry joined in as the editor – thank you for the editorial assistance and the care in listening to my vision (even defending it). At Wits University Press, I am grateful to Roshan Cader for those moments when she was patient with the delays and difficulties of writing a book during the height of South Africa's lockdown regulations and the uncertainty that came with the Covid-19 pandemic.

Xander Ehlers not only assisted in conducting the fieldwork in Bethal but became my interlocutor. Thank you! Bab' William Matlatla, I am grateful to have an elder like you, who always shares his knowledge. Thank you for linking me up with Xander. I hope to keep my promise to take you to Bethal one day.

As a student, I had teachers who inspired me. I did not encounter these teachers in the classroom only; they taught me some valuable lessons outside the classroom too. Today I have the privilege of calling some of these teachers friends and colleagues. I am grateful for the spirit that drove them to be patient with me even when I did not make sense.

At Wits University, I am thankful for the support from Prishani Naidoo, director of the Society, Work and Politics Institute (SWOP), who always lent an ear and a hand when I needed assistance. Thanks also to Ingrid Chunilall, Josephine Mashaba, Sedzani Malada and Lucinda Becorny for always being there when I needed to speak to someone. At SWOP, thank you to Dineo Skosana, Tasneem Essop and Brittany Kesselman. I am grateful to Thabang Sefalala, who dedicated his time a decade ago and drove me to farms in Gauteng. Thanks for the intellectual conversations that started many years ago with Marxism and the failed promise of a coming revolution. Thanks to Bridget Kenny for reminding me that I have something to contribute and for the slots she always makes available for me to teach her students.

A decade ago, I had a chance to work with Eddie Webster, who introduced me to the issues faced by farmworkers. When our paths crossed, my life changed! Madala, I am grateful for the care you have shown to the generations with whom you have shared your knowledge. Your generosity is something I will share with my students.

I would also like to express my gratitude to Gillian Hart for always availing herself and providing critical interventions relating to 'praxis' in my academic work. Thanks to Karl von Holdt for the professorial bag – my challenge now is to prove that it is possible to become a professor within the next five years.

I also thank my friends who keep reminding me that friendship is about reflecting the good in each other, reciprocity, generosity and care: Themba Tshabalala, Nhlanhla Lucky (Jojo) Radebe, Issac Ntuli, (soon to be Dr) Musawenkosi Malabela, Khethukuthula Jele, Bongani (Mzambiya) Ngwenya, Falakhe Sibiya (RIP), Nonkuleko Mabaso, Fikile Masikane, Nelisiwe Mkhele, Katlego Ramatsima, Popopo Mohala, Innocentia Kgapola, Nompumelelo Melaphi, Uyabongeka Walaza, Nolundi Walaza, Nicolas Pons-Vignon, Sizwe Mbatha, Bhabhali ka Maphikela Nhlapho and Gift Sonkqayi.

Yandisa Khonziwe Lutricia Sosibo, my special orchid, thanks for travelling to Wits with me all those nights when we were dealing with the lockdown curfew, trying to ensure we were on the right side of the law while we finished our respective academic projects. And thanks for reminding me of the power of prayer, even though you had to sleep on your knees one night. It was on that night that I fell in love with you.

At the end of my writing journey, I joined the University of Pretoria as a lecturer in the Department of Sociology, and I am grateful for the encouragement and assistance from my colleagues: Debby Bonin, Zitha Mokomane, Sepetla Molapo, Vangile Bingma, Charles Puttergill, Alf Nilsen, Tshwarelo Sekhaulelo and Neo Mohlabane.

To write this book was to walk with unquantifiable matter, abaphansi. These are ancestors who made a demand to write about them. They haunted me as I had to create and make a home for myself. A home not only in the physical state of an abode, but an eternal coming home! Ngiyabonga Somandla!

Prologue | Emazambaneni: The land of terror

Imagine that you are lost in a twisted world with no one to depend on. When you bleed, no matter how much you shout and scream, no one comes. All you have is hope – hope that someone will hear your cry and that salvation will come. Hope that someone will at least recognise you as a human being, with blood and life in your veins.

Then imagine that this is not some imaginary world you've been thrown into. It is your world. It is your home. Not only this, but history reminds you that you are linked to great ancestors who once lived in it.

Now bring the land into closer focus – farmland in the region of the Eastern Transvaal (now Mpumalanga), South Africa, and a small rural town named Bethal.

It is here where, in 1954, an unidentified man takes 'a great opportunity to write ... these few lines ...' His letter is intended for the head of the Department of Prisons in Pretoria and he is writing from Leslie jail, on behalf of himself and his fellow inmates. By doing so he is risking his life.

In fact, it is not a letter: it is a desperate plea. The terror is palpable. The struggle to hold on to the little breath of life that might get snatched away is evident in every line (see figure 0.1).

This letter was one of the first things I read about Bethal when I was working on my PhD research project. It lies in the Historical Papers Research Archive at Wits University, the accompanying information being that it was smuggled out of the jail and into the hands of

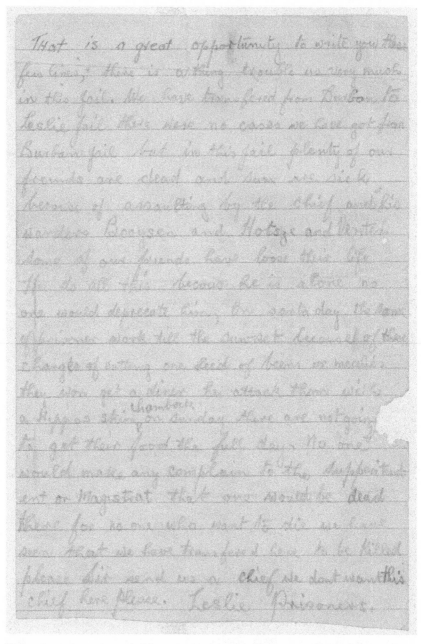

Figure 0.1: A letter smuggled from Leslie jail addressed to the Department of Prisons in Pretoria. The author is unknown – he is writing on behalf of himself and his fellow inmates, detailing the brutality of working on potato farms in Bethal. (Historical Papers Research Archive, University of the Witwatersrand, South Africa)

we get three meat every sunday
no Hospital for the sick prisoners they
dont get any madicine they cured by
God. They carry big stones on their
shoulders attacking and assaulting them
with bumboo cane or knobkerry
up & down with chief & prisoner
& at the dinner time we get one cup of
mealies and full up with water
on wednesday and sunday we eat
meat which is dead for to self a dirty
and smell, we dont know where did
they get this meat just like.
But we can't made any complain
to the new suppentend because
of we are going to be killed after
he head you —

address:— The Head Office
prisonment
Pretoria T.V.L.

William Barney Ngakane, who shared it with Henri-Philippe Junod on 15 March 1954.

In the 1950s, the spotlight in South African history shifted from resistance politics in the urban areas to a scandal in this small rural town. The area, which was known for potato farming, was called 'emazambaneni' (the land of potatoes) by the workers and the community members, and there was a song they sang: 'khona le eBethal siyoghuba amazambane' (there in Bethal where we will be digging potatoes). The song aimed to capture the brutality and violence that was happening on the Bethal potato farms.

This violence was not new, however. In November 1951, some years before the letter was written, an inquest into farm violence found that a person called Phivi and two other labourers were so terrified upon learning that the train they were on was taking them to Bethal – and not, as they had been told, to Germiston – that they jumped off the train. In his attempt to escape this fate, Phivi was killed.

The prisoner's letter is reproduced in figure 0.1, but I have recorded it again here, so that you may read it in the light of the above and hold it in your mind.

> That is a great opportunity to write you these few lines, there is a thing trouble us very much in this jail. We have transferred from Durban to Leslie Jail there were no cases we have got from Durban Jail but in this Jail plenty of our friends are dead and sum are sick because of assaulting by the chief and his warders Booysen and Hotsze and Venter Some of our friends have loose their life He do all this because he is alone no one would deprecate him, On sartady the some of prisoner work till the sun-set because of their charges of cutting one seed of beens or mealies they won get a diner he attack them with a Hippos skin chambok on Sunday there are not going to get their food the full day, No one would make any complain to the Supperintendent or Magistrat that one would be dead there for no one who want to die we have seen that we have

transferred here to be killed please Sir send us a chief we dont want this chief here please. Leslie Prisoners.

We get three meals every Sundays no Hospital for the sick prisoners. they dont gey any madicine they cured by God. They carry big stones on their shoulders attacking and assaulting them with bamboo cane or Knob Kerry up + down with chief and prisoner at the diner time we get one cup of mealies and full up with water on Wednesday and Sunday we eat meat which is dead for its self a dirty and smell we dont know where did they get this meat just like. but we cant make any complain to the new Supperitend because of we are going to be killed after he had gon.

Address: The Head Office
Prisonerment
Pritoria T.V.L. [sic][1]

Emazambaneni – the land of violence and white terror – is starkly captured in this prison labourer's words, expressing his urgent desire to be free from it. Ngakane was employed as a field relations officer by the South African Institute of Race Relations (SAIRR) in the 1950s, and Junod was the national organiser of the Penal Reform League in South Africa. Ngakane's intention in sharing the letter with Junod was to raise awareness about the plight of prison labourers in Bethal, in the hope that the Penal Reform League would carry the matter forward with the Minister of Justice.

At the time I encountered the historical archive on Bethal, I was facing methodological challenges in my PhD project because a white farmer had decided not to keep to our arrangement and allow me to conduct ethnographic research on his farm. The PhD was on rethinking resistance with a focus on the everyday experiences of farmworkers. I wanted to understand what forms of resistance and engagement farmworkers in Gauteng province participate in to effect change in their individual and collective lives. The intention was to conduct an ethnographic study on a large farm that employed over 100 workers in Germiston. The ethnography would have entailed my working there as a farmworker.

I had been due to begin the fieldwork in February 2016. After the rejection from the farmer, in my disappointment I confided in Mam Winnie (not her real name), a farmworker with whom I had been in regular contact since 2012 regarding her experiences of working on the farm. Her words resonated and remained with me, and they influenced the trajectory of my thesis. 'To understand yourself and your project,' Mam Winnie said, 'you have to study me. It is through your relationship with me that you will begin to understand the truth about yourself and your study.'

I tried to find ways to deal with two things – the resistance of farmworkers in South African history and the violence in agriculture in South Africa. I selected Bethal as a historical site to make a general argument about agriculture in South Africa. Why did I study Bethal? In 2012, when I was an intern at the Society, Work and Politics Institute (SWOP) under the mentorship of Professor Eddie Webster, we were writing a report for the Gauteng Department of Economic Development at his house when Professor Luli Callinicos told me about Gert Sibande and the potato boycott in Bethal.

Strangely, all of this was at the back of my mind when, in 2017, I went to the Historical Papers Research Archive with no specific research question in mind. When I opened the box given to me by the archivist – box number 12, AD 1947/25.1–25.6 Farm Labour – I had no clue what to look for or research. I decided to open the files randomly. I started with file number 25.3.

The letter from the unidentified prison labourer was the first document I read. I felt that the letter was addressed to me, inviting me to see for myself, through this prisoner's eyes, the hopeless despair of his situation.

The trouble with the eye is that it cannot see itself. In Shakespeare's *Julius Caesar*, Brutus tells Cassius that 'the eye sees not itself / But by reflection, by some other things'.[2] The invitation to me from Mam Winnie was to see through her reflection as an act of seeing myself: 'Ukubona mina njengo mama wakho ukuzibona wena'[3] (To see me as your mother is to see yourself). 'For your project to be successful, you must see me as an act of seeing yourself.' This was not only a metaphysical intervention but a methodological one as well. To see and read the letter was to see myself as well.

It was also through Mam Winnie that I became aware of the violence in agriculture when, in May 2012, the farmer she was working for assaulted her. After hearing of this assault, Eddie, myself and a trade unionist in the agricultural sector accompanied her to the police station to open a case. The trade unionist said she was used to hearing about violence on farms; they were currently dealing with a criminal case in the same area where the farmer had made workers lift heavy rocks.

When I read the letter by the Bethal prison labourer in 2017, I was reminded of this incident, especially the fact that the prisoners were made to pick up rocks as a form of punishment.

An 'opportunity to write' represented an opportunity for me: to write of justice, the past, the present and the future. After interacting with Mam Winnie and then reading the prison labourer's letter, I was never the same. I was haunted by the feeling that there was a demand to write of this history but I didn't yet know how I might do that. I addressed my encounter with Mam Winnie at PhD level, but after attaining my doctorate, I felt that the issue of the Bethal letter could not remain as simply some minor academic footnote in the various essays I wrote in the course of completing my thesis. The questions I had were similar to the questions I had had when Mam Winnie invited me to see my life through hers. Was I going to write about Bethal as if I did not feel that I had an affinity with the author of the letter? I felt that I knew him, that he was a part of my future.

When I decided to write a book about Bethal, I went back to the letter. It was making a different demand on me. It required me to remember my past and brought me back to my starting point: land, labour and resistance. In my many readings of the letter, I imagined the laborious effort this prisoner would have gone through in writing it and the fears he would have had about getting caught out. Punishment would have been severe – it could have got him killed. I felt that the author wasn't just addressing those in the past but was addressing me directly. I wondered what had happened to this man. I searched in vain for his name or some other way of discovering who he was or whether he ever received any assistance. How old was he? What had he hoped to achieve by writing the letter?

Ralph Ellison wrote, 'History makes harsh demands of us all,'[4] while W.E.B. Du Bois observed that to respond to the demands made by history on the individual, 'there must be … some standards of ethics in research and interpretations'.[5] In my practice of writing and researching, I wanted to locate myself in this disoriented, dislocated, distorted reality, and deliberate my actions. Action is grounded in morality. And once we touch the subject of morality, the ethereal subject of justice emerges.

The letter reveals what was supposed to be hidden and goes against the omnipresent power of the farmer. It invites one to reflect on life in Bethal under the tyranny of the minority wielding weapons that would be turned against them in the future.

Those who occupy the Black skin are said to be a 'captive body', thrown into a world of unrelieved crisis, and sometimes their actions of being recognised as bodies that are part of humanity are said to have no significance.[6] Living distorted lives, they cannot attain the status of being human. In my PhD dissertation, I argue that justice is the product of the future and belongs to the dead. Jacques Derrida said that 'truth is spectral',[7] but in South Africa who does it haunt? Death is a societal scandal, for the way we die absolves us from the life we lived – for in living, we were anonymous, invisible and nameless.[8] The dead are immortalised through reports that scandalise their ways of attempting to survive. The writing does not celebrate death but is a criticism of not-living, a manifesto towards life in the land. Emmanuel Levinas warns us about the dangers of violence:

The trial by force is the test of the real. But violence does not consist so much in injuring and annihilating persons as in interrupting their continuity, making them play roles in which they no longer recognize themselves, making them betray not only commitments but their own substance … every war employs arms that turn against those who wield them.[9]

When I read the prisoner's letter and considered my interaction with Mam Winnie, I was confused, not understanding whether I was looking at the past or the present. This distorted reality, this subject in crisis, this Other, who is distant to me, is part and parcel of a reality that is constantly turning, especially towards those who wield arms to claim the future. I saw this as an invitation to deliberate on the actions of the researcher studying their community. Linda Smith, in *Decolonizing Methodologies*,[10] argues that the challenge of a researcher emerging from the history of coloniality is no longer about a search for an 'Other'. To Smith, decolonised research is about drawing axiological lessons about values and principles from the community one is studying. Thus, this book attempts to bring forward ethical lessons for the future.

As shown in the letter, violence is used to ensure that workers do not challenge the farmer in future. The future, for violence, is always in a state of precarity. Today it may get its ends, but the future remains unknown to it. The law aims to fashion a particular social order that justifies the use of violence.[11] Every social order aims to conceal an anxiety about the unknown future.

The futurity of violence

In thinking of the future, I thought of our present time, which bears the unresolved scars of the past, where Black people still do not have a place of peace, a place of rest, in the country of their birth. That is why I had to return to Bethal, historically and in the present. I wondered what Bethal looks like in the twenty-first century. What does the future of the land look like in Bethal today?

In answering the question, I show how violence operates, and I present something unknown to every actor involved in Bethal: the future. The acts of violence go beyond the present or the past. In South Africa we can use the example where the 'former' oppressor responds ferociously when the 'former' oppressed indicates the importance of addressing the issue of land dispossession. The response is almost always that Black farmworkers must forget about the past and its viciousness, especially considering that today South Africa 'is not a predominantly agrarian society'.[12] The unjust violence of dispossession and land redistribution ends up being seen from a materialistic viewpoint, meaning that the land related to past injustices is important only if it solves the material issues. As if during the colonial encounter, Black people suffered only material loss.

This approach misses the point about the futurity of violence. Violence is an extremely headstrong lover whose preferred partner is docility. The prisoner's letter illustrates this graphically. The purpose and intention of violent acts is to shape a generation of docile beings. In resorting to violence, the farmer is looking to thwart future resistance. To use violence is to seek to have a hand in controlling the unknown future and its possibilities.

How crime is handled reflects the state of the common conscience of a particular society,[13] but what does it reveal about South Africa during apartheid? I have indicated that how violence is deployed also reveals the law it seeks to create.[14] Thus, in dealing with the law and violence, we understand the type of social order that is fashioned. The principle is violence + law = social order.[15] The use of violence also reflects the future that each social order intends to secure in the now. This future is terrifying because, as the writer of the letter is aware, '[n]o one would make any complain to the Supperintendent or Magistrat that one would be dead'. This line clarifies my formulation of violence and social order. The violence captured by the letter reflects not only the conditions on the farm but also the social order at large. In looking at violence and law, I contend that violence as law-making is about securing the unknown future.

Chapter 1 | The spectre of the human potato

It was revealed how on the potato farms, as they were digging potatoes using ploughs pulled by cows, a dead person – a human body –
was discovered. Again when the lorries arrived in Johannesburg it
was reported that in one of the potato bags appeared a human head
instead of a potato. But I for one I never saw it. I just heard when I
arrived at eGoli [Johannesburg]. It was then that the quarrel began.
People in Johannesburg started accusing us of killing people and
planting them as potatoes. When we arrived in Johannesburg they
would say, 'Yes, we saw a potato that looked like a human being from
the farm you were working on. You are the ones who were beating
up these people, you guards.' — Ngubeza Mahlangu[1]

Ngubeza Mahlangu's statement, which he made in an interview with
Tshepo Moloi that took place in eMzinoni, Bethal (Mpumalanga),
on 4 August 2008, speaks to a particular time in South African history.

When a human head was found amid a potato crop in 1959, it sparked
a rallying call for political action: to boycott the buying and consumption
of potatoes. At the time, many claimed to see potatoes that looked like
'human beings' sold in markets across South Africa. The sacks of potatoes were traced back to farms around Bethal. On 31 May of that year,
the last day of the two-day national conference of the African National
Congress (ANC), the activist Robert Resha 'called for a boycott of potatoes to begin at midnight as a new protest against bestial treatment of

African farm laborers'.[2] The call was supported by the South African Congress of Trade Unions (SACTU). Moses Mabhida, the acting president of the ANC in Natal, argued that '[t] he potato boycott was the first direct attack on one of the main pillars of reactionary policies in our country, namely, the feudal farming interests. The main economic base of the South African cheap labour structure, with its pass laws, migratory labour, low wages, is the twin pillar of mining and farming interests.'[3]

The 'human potato' haunted the South African landscape in the 1940s and 1950s. Newspapers reported how farmers in Bethal were brutally killing farmworkers, secretly burying them in unmarked graves on the farms. One worker told of seeing a plough dig up skulls and bones when he and others were working the land.[4] The spectre of a human potato was the coming back to light of unseen deeds, of acts committed by farmers and exposed by journalists and activists such as Gert Sibande, Henry Nxumalo, Ruth First, Reverend Michael Scott and William Barney Ngakane,[5] revealing how the state was implicated through its passing of the 'petty offenders' scheme', whereby Black people guilty of 'petty' apartheid crimes – such as not having the notorious apartheid pass – found themselves working on the farms around Bethal.

The petty offenders' scheme was a way for the government to deal simultaneously with the shortage of labour on farms and the overcrowding in prisons. The origin of the scheme can be traced back to an arrangement piloted in 1947 by P.J. de Beer, a public prosecutor at the Native Commissioner's court in Fordsburg, Johannesburg. It became official from 1953. The scheme stipulated that Black people who broke the law (for petty crimes mostly) had to serve time in prison for three months or 'volunteer' to work on the farms for one to two shillings a day. Deborah Posel shows that by 1957/1958 about 200 000 prison labourers worked on farms.[6]

Newspaper reports covering the reasons behind the potato boycott meant that the violence on the farms and the exploitation of the cheap labour of Black people were publicly exposed.

What remains unanswered is how a potato ended up looking like a human being and how one makes sense of something like this. It requires an eye that sees beyond material logic, an eye that apprehends the work of the spirit. The potato that looked like a human was seen as the spiritual return of a dead worker, embodying that which was buried in the land, the worker brutally killed by the farmer. The spectre of the 'human' potato is an invitation to perceive the spiritual. To see through the spiritual eye is to confront this episode in South African history.

In his article 'Bethal Today: *Drum's* Fearless Exposure of Human Exploitation', *Drum* journalist Henry Nxumalo revealed that the contract workers and prison labourers in Bethal were clothed in sacks made from potato bags. They slept on these sacks and even used them as dishes for their food. When one looked from afar at labourers working the fields, one would see potato sacks, but inside those sacks were humans, using the sacks to cover their naked bodies. The potato sack was also worn by 'difficult' workers or those who attempted to escape from the farm. It was hardly a warm item of clothing – and northern Bethal, where most potato farming took place, was known for its cold weather, especially at night. Forcing farm labourers to don hessian sacks was another way of dehumanising them, treating them as if they were literally 'sacks of potatoes' without any dignity (see figure 1.1).

Farmers punished their workers arbitrarily. The *Drum* exposé considered this 'arbitrary punishment' irrational since the farmers had complained that they needed workers. It was shocking that farmers could complain about a labour shortage and yet kill the workers they said they needed. Sentencing a farmer in Delmas to five years in prison, the judge who presided over that case said it was 'a great scandal and one which may still have a very serious result on racial relations in this country'.[7] But why should this violence be a racial problem? What does it reveal and what does it conceal? To subject the Other to violence does not only seek to eliminate them; it also seeks to conceal the anxiety of the one who uses the violence. I see this violence as expressing not just the anxiety of the farmer. I see it as speaking directly of the fears of a white

Figure 1.1: A team of workers working the fields, some of them wearing clothes made from potato sacks, Bethal, 1952. (Photo by Jürgen Schadeberg from the Schadeberg Collection)

society that perceived itself as a minority in a country of ungovernable natives. This fear presented itself through the 'native question' – that is to say that white people could not dominate the land and the labour power of the natives without being met by resistance in the future.[8]

I look at history through the eyes of this human potato as the pivotal point in unpacking and understanding the happenings on the Bethal farms and in farm prisons – the eye as heuristic model, in other words. Through this method we uncover the meaning of the potato that came back looking like a human. The human potato – murdered, buried – was the culmination of state-regulated forced labour, sanctioned coercion administered in various ways, including laws that rendered many Black people homeless. The potato that haunted South Africa at the time complicated how the potato was understood. In the morphology of potatoes, they have 'eyes', tubers or nodes from which new potato plants sprout. It was as though the potato was positioned in such a way as to be looking up from deep beneath the soil, its eyes seeing the violations that were taking place on the farms. Then the potato was not a neutral commodity, for it had eyes that witnessed the injustices. It even took on the shape of the dead people that it encountered in the soil and became a commodity used to demand justice for the dead human potato, an aberration that haunted the Union of South Africa. People stopped eating potatoes, demanding justice for all the farmworkers in the Eastern Transvaal.

Frances Baard, unionist and founding member of the ANC Women's League (ANCWL), reflected on the potato boycott in her book *My Spirit Is Not Banned*:

> We used to condemn a potato when we see one that had a hole or a black mark. We used to tell the people in the public meetings, 'you see this mark here? It's where your child's blood went in. You see this mark here? It's the blood of our children, that's why the potato is so.'
>
> The people started hating potatoes like anything. And even the whites when they heard that we are boycotting the potatoes and that we say that these potatoes are full of the blood of the African people, then they also began boycotting them. That boycott was very effective you know. The farmers couldn't sell their potatoes anywhere, and at the market the workers wouldn't even carry the potatoes.[9]

Baard was likely pointing to the eyes of the potato (the sprouts), and through these markings she and other activists used the potato as a symbol of social justice for the dead and violated. Some, who did not see the human potato in reality, used their mind's eye. Others believed that they had actually seen a human potato. By using the 'eyes' of the potato as organs of seeing, the boycott organisers called many to action, as it was believed that 'on the blood and bones of these bewildered prisoners and workers grew the potatoes on which the populace fed' (see figure 1.2).[10]

The eschatological eye is what organises this book – it is a call to see with a spiritual eye – and its writing is 'Otherwise'. The historical material collected through the archives and interviews with workers from the period is presented in a manner that aims to offer a material view of the brutality suffered by those who worked the land in this small farming community. To write Otherwise is to use the eyes of the Other to uncover the meaning of the period. This form of writing is about alterity. I look at cases from the 1940s to the 1960s (subsequent to the

Figure 1.2: In 1959, during the period of the potato boycott, ANC activists carry a coffin with potatoes on top of it to the graveside. Staging a reminder of the injustices on potato farms, the coffin bearers wear hessian potato sacks and necklaces made from potatoes. (BAHA/Africa Media Online)

boycott and exposé). I then travel to the present to look into the memory of the violence in Bethal by reading transcripts of interviews conducted in 2008 with the children of labour tenants who experienced life on the farm during the violence. I present the book as a history that remains present with us. In order to do this I visited Bethal in 2020 and 2021 and looked into what it means to write of 'Bethal today'.

In writing about Bethal and the brutality in this land, my aim is to reveal how land ownership and private property (such as the farm) are linked to violence and contestation. To present this contestation historically, the gaze alternates from the eyes of the farmworkers to the eyes of the farmer who petitioned the state to acquire more labour to work the land and complained that, because Black people did not like this kind of work, it was hard to keep them from leaving the farms. At the same time, this farmer is the one responsible for the deaths of the farmworkers. The eyes of the farmer are the eyes of authority, and such eyes usually seek to conceal rather than reveal. In the eyes of authority, the problem was one of material loss as the potatoes were not eaten and were rotting. In the eyes of authority, the human potato never existed. What existed were workers who did not want to work and who had to be subjected to violence to accept the conditions on the farm. Through this alternation, my aim is to see the anxiety presented as 'ontological nowhereness' experienced by the workers.

The mere presence of Black workers in large numbers on the farm was enough to create the anxiety of 'swart gevaar' for the farmer. The great contradiction of the petty offenders' scheme was that it brought to the farm not a mere labourer but also a 'criminal' to work the land.

Violence and the meaning of land

The farm is a violent site in South African history. During apartheid, several activists who were caught by the state disappeared and died on state-owned farms after long periods of violent interrogation.[11] But farms had long been places of violence, as seen during the period of the Anglo-Boer War (1899–1902) and the scorched-earth policy[12] of Lord Kitchener. This resulted in the deaths of many Afrikaners, a cause for severe trauma in their memory as they discovered scores of dead Afrikaners on farms. They vowed that never again would they be separated from the 'platteland'.[13] The Afrikaners argued that it was through this land, also called 'plaatland', that they were linked to their ancestors who had defied colonial invasion by the British. The Anglo-Boer War accelerated nationalism, which fuelled the desire to create a land that would allow the Afrikaner to mourn.[14] Afrikaner domination, which expressed itself racially, was about psychological superiority, which can be traced to the Afrikaner commandos who subscribed to the view that land ownership was determined according to blood/inheritance. Others were to add that the violence of nationalism was directed towards those who were deemed inferior and fuelled a spirit of defiance against the English, the colonisers.[15] Those who were inferior, it was justified, were of a weaker blood and could not rule the land. The argument by this scholarship went as follows:

> The roots of apartheid are to be found not in the white cities, nor even in the endless tunnels of the gold mines of the Rand. They are buried deep in the red soil of the white-owned farms, where for some two hundred years, before even South Africa became an urban industrial economy and the word apartheid was thought of, relationships were being forged between white masters and black servants.[16]

At the core of the violence of dispossession is the loss that Black generations suffered. In the colonial encounter they not only lost their land, they lost their entire being. They were removed from the land owned by their ancestors and then treated like slaves by the white society.

In metaphysics, ontology is a branch of philosophy concerned with being. A Black person is linked ontologically and eschatologically to the land, beginning with the burying of the umbilical cord after the birth of a child, thereby giving oneself to the land. This is considered to be the most important act in any child's life, and with it comes the instruction 'uwuhloniphe lomhlaba ngoba ilapho inkaba yakho ikhona' (respect this land for it is where your umbilical cord is). Within this practice, either a tree is planted where the umbilical cord is buried or the cord is buried under a family tree that was planted long ago. In the future, when that person dies, a branch from the same tree is used to fetch their spirit from the place where they died, so that it may be returned to where they were born.

This is the first ethical relationship that Black people establish with the land. This ethical relationship goes beyond respect for the land itself;

it speaks to the living and the dead, for all people come from the land and will return to the land. Dispossession destroys this link with the land. When people are forcibly removed from the land, they leave behind not only their umbilical cords but the graves of their ancestors as well.

Dispossession made most Black people belong nowhere: this is what I call ontological nowhereness. This trauma of ontological nowhereness is best described by Solomon Plaatje in his retelling of how the 1913 Land Act made Black people 'pariahs' in the land where they were born and even subjected their animals to cruelty.[17] By being dispossessed, Black people had no place they could call home; they had to wander to other areas in search of a home. Their dispossession also meant that they had no place to bury their dead since they had left the graves of their ancestors behind. Plaatje argued that if we are to total the number of victims of the violent law of the Union that forced many to be without a home, we must add the cattle:

> We frequently met those roving pariahs, with their hungry cattle, and wondered if the animals were not more deserving of pity than their owners. It may be the cattle's misfortune that they have a black owner, but it is certainly not their fault, for sheep have no choice in the selection of a colour for their owners, and no cows or goats are ever asked to decide if the black boy who milks them shall be their owner, or but a herd[er] in the employ of a white man; so why should they be starved on account of the colour of their owners? We knew of a law to prevent cruelty to animals, but had never thought that we should live to meet in one day so many dumb creatures making silent appeals to Heaven for protection against the law.[18]

The vast hectares of land owned by the white farmer are marked by violence and death. This is the nature of dispossession. The potato that looked like a human gave an account of the brutality of the ontological nowhereness of the Black person. This brutality reveals the nature of dispossession and the resilience of those working the land. Such resilience involves a spiritual look at the land, what I call an eschatological gaze, whereby the Black workers saw the land as their home, a future for their children, a place where they would be buried in peace and transition to be with their ancestors.

In researching the historical archives, one is always already dealing with a problem of representation, of making the forgotten remembered and the remembered forgotten again. The value of writing this archive Otherwise is in its silence(s), its (re)presentation of the presence of the past, of the preoccupation with the past from which the present has demanded a future. To write Otherwise is to recognise alterity. In phenomenology, alterity is not shunned. There is always an Other who exists outside of one's self. Dealing with alterity in knowledge production does not mean to use the language of morality or that this form of knowledge is wrong. The issue is that we cannot assume to take the position of the Other, or to speak for the Other, or to take the space of the Other, while we have acknowledged that they are an Other.[19]

The historical archive I researched speaks of/for an Other. In this case, it is the violated Black person who despises exploitative farm work but loves the land because it carries meaning (their home, a place that feeds them, a place to lay their dead bodies in future). The archive I consulted is the Historical Papers Research Archive housed at the University of the Witwatersrand. As the official repository of the South African Institute of Race Relations (SAIRR), among other institutions and organisations, this archive is a storehouse of letters shared amongst individuals (from the 1940s to the 1960s), responses from the state (for example, through the Secretary of Native Affairs), various newspaper clippings, policy documents and minutes from meetings. This material is not focused exclusively on the Bethal region but gives a nuanced understanding of South Africa's agricultural sector as a whole.

In dealing with the archive, we are already confronting the problem of violence and the violence of representation, a violence that was speaking to and constructing how the Other is and how the Other ought to be treated. In writing the archive Otherwise, I will not be discussing whether the representation of the problems of the past was correct; my interest is the question of the future of violence. In writing Otherwise, I offer a philosophical understanding of the ethical relationship with land established by the dispossessed and I engage with important questions. How does the trek caused by dispossession help us understand what became an imminent confrontation with death? What does this question of death tell us?

The farm and the question of land has made a return in our present: we see this in the public discourse of the land debate as expropriation without compensation, which thus returns us to the violent nature of dispossession. To the farmers, this debate is seen as inciting violence. Farmers are suspicious of the democratic government and blame it for failing to protect them in what is falsely claimed to be a white genocide in South Africa.[20] While the public debate is focused on land expropriation without compensation, there is a neglect of how private property in South Africa is constructed as a terrain of the father (in this case white) and how the father is willing to use violence to protect that property. In studying everyday life on the farm, we come to understand that land ownership was not only economic. It also came with the ownership of many souls that resided on the farm, and the farmer became the law and the police officer. This was said to be a tradition of paternalism.[21]

The idea of paternalism is traced back to the violent relations during the period of slavery, when the master depended on violence and a 'discourse that tried to define slaves' labour as a legitimate return for their masters' protection'.[22] Scholars attribute the emergence of paternalism to the Cape wine farms in the nineteenth century, when, as pressure mounted for the abolition of slavery, the farmers styled themselves as the father, giving a new master-and-servant relationship that denied the independence of those termed children.[23] Andries du Toit argued that this view drew on eighteenth-century Europe, which emphasised the master's despotic powers over their child (the servant). The idea of paternalism draws on a patriarchal family structure: the farm is seen as a family unit in which the white landowner becomes the father to all those who are staying and offering their labour on his farm over many generations. The women have it worse since they have no authority but must obey their brother in the household, who will take over the role of the father, and their white father, who controls the entire family structure.

The labour power is for the service of the white father first. This relationship is usually violent, with the farmer using a whip to discipline his children or employing his symbolic power, which aims continually to infantilise the servants by giving them names that suggest they are children. The concept of paternalism does not reveal why the workers are perpetually treated like children. Why does the farmer use violence to discipline them? This is linked to private property and the future of land ownership. To infantilise the workers is to ensure that they remain in the service of the farmer and do not contest his possession of the land. Paternalism ensures that the authority of the farmer is not questioned.

To see through the eyes of the workers in Bethal is to see beyond violence and perceive the nature of private property. The creation of private property is a violent process and to see the farm as indicated is to see the untold violence of the South African historical present.

Seeing beyond violence

The point being made is that private property conceals the anxious father who uses violence not just to thwart resistance but also to conceal the illegitimate status of fatherhood that rests on the idea of private property. This means that seeing the question of land through the idea of property limits our appreciation of what it means to belong to the land. What do I mean? Private property creates an ontological existence that always sees land as that which can be owned. And if it can be owned, then it can be protected – and that protection is done through violence. The securing of the future through violence aims to allow for private property to continue and to prevent any rebellion that might unmask the precarious position occupied by the father. That is why even the silent are suspected and are killed (as was the case in Bethal). The spectre of the human potato revealed the ontological fragility and anxiety of the farmers' claims to the land through violence.

The eschatological future

The conditions in Bethal make clear that in those times the white farmers felt threatened by those who were criminalised by the apartheid system. In today's South Africa, the threat to the white farmer comes from Black farmworkers/labour tenants who have rights, from the unknown criminal who is responsible for the 'white genocide' and from a state tasked with defending the rights of its citizens. The way ownership is conceived creates anxiety in the white farming community, and this anxiety is always related to the unknown eschatological future – the fear that the 'owners' might lose their claim to the land and the graves of their ancestors. Violence is used, therefore, first as an ontological claim (that the 'owners' belong to the land rightfully) and to secure a future home (but only for themselves). What remains unsolved in this story is the future of the Black farmworkers who are still facing the violence and earning next to nothing. Where does the Black farmworker belong in this land? As long as this question remains unsolved, the future of the land remains contested. The spirit of this land will continue to demand justice for the nameless Black farmworkers buried in the soil.

Overview of the chapters that follow

In chapter 2, 'Whose eyes are looking at history?', I theorise the importance of asking whose eyes are looking at the anguish of the dispossessed. I theorise how the eye is not just about seeing; it is an ethical organ that hears, and recognises, the face of the Other.[24] This is a phenomenological theorisation of the eye. I map out the eye as a prejudiced organ and bring forth a puzzle: how can we appreciate history through the eye if the eye is an organ of prejudice? If we are to solve this puzzle and thus ascertain the meaning of this period, the question of whose eyes are looking at the history of the dispossessed becomes important.

I argue that the eye of the dominant sees the Other differently. It misrecognises the dominated. I implicate the eye as a central organ that dominated how the oppression of farmworkers was perceived. First, we see through the eyes of the dominant, specifically the eyes of one P.J. de Beer at the Fordsburg Native Commissioner's court, who argued that farm work was good for Black prisoners – despite the rumours that farmers were murdering Black people on the farms. The eyes of the dominant dominate the archive, but they also betray and ridicule them. Authority tends to ridicule those in power and the case of De Beer is *locus classicus*. In an investigation into how the petty offenders' scheme was applied, De Beer was charged with corruption when it was revealed that he had keys to a truck that transported prison labourers to a Bethal farm. De Beer was not blind to what was happening on the farms in Bethal. That is why, later, we see the human potato as not only haunting those in power, but also ridiculing them for thinking that they could conceal murder.

Through the eyes of human potatoes, we excavate the truth of the dead and the suffering of the living. This suffering is located on the farms where labourers worked and whose land was owned by white farmers. The workers looked at the land they toiled with an eschato-logical gaze, which involves looking at the land through a spiritual eye. This is a process of assessing the land through its aggregating sufferings endured by the farmworkers, and treating these sufferings as indicative of the farmworkers' pending deaths – because the farm was integral to the killings of the farmworkers. At the same time, Black people have always had a bodily and spiritual bond with the eschatological world of their ancestors, and this made the living farmworkers believe that in the end the dead would find rest in this land.

This period of dispossession is seen through the eyes of farmworkers who were searching for a home and who confronted death in a hidden space called the farm. Not only did they work that land, but that land was also a home, because they could not go anywhere else. The spiritual significance of land is often forgotten. Through the farmworkers' eyes, we realise that land is involved in the cycle of life and is also the driving force of spirituality.

The potato has an interesting social, economic and political history. Domesticated in the Andean region,[25] it bears the tragic history of mass starvation in Ireland, and then the South African story of a potato that looked like a human, in a small town called Bethal. Potato farming in this area is said to have been introduced by the Jews who migrated to South Africa around 1910.

Chapter 3, 'Bethal, the house of God', shows the violence that was unleashed on those who worked the land, the individual as well as mass killings, and the remains that were discarded unashamedly or buried like those of dogs. Such gruesome events on the farms were normal. Behind this violence is the figure of a white farmer who petitions the state for more farm labour, accusing the Black worker of loathing farm work and of desertion. This petition to the state for more farm labour conceals the pain of the Black farmworkers, their violent deaths and indecent burial, and the brutality of being homeless and not belonging anywhere in South Africa. Those who escaped the system were confronted with what I call the pain of ontological nowhereness. If they ran away from the white father on the farm, they were still confronted by the state that wanted to know where they belonged (the use of the apartheid pass), and if they had no proof, they were sent to prison and then back to the farms.

The farmers who killed farmworkers were forced in a court of law to speak the truth about their killings, in a show-and-tell, and the violated Black workers were supposed to gain their 'justice'. But this form of justice did not to speak to the problem. The farmer did not confess; he still kept the land and returned to his home. We do not know what rested heavily on the conscience of the farmer, but on the land the injustice was exposed by the human potato. The ultimate violence inflicted on those dispossessed was their deaths: the cruelty of having their graves dug by other workers, being buried like dogs, with the added insult of no one informing their families; instead they were reported as missing or having disappeared. That they were stripped of their birthright of being returned to the land when dead is the worst form of violence against the farmworkers. That is why many fled, in the hope that they would find a better place to be buried and be returned to their land peacefully.

The usage of violence has consequences. It also shapes the subjectivity of those who kill. It remains in their spirit and distorts their view of the world. The only way to continue living is to continue with the urge to kill. I use the Zulu word 'iqunga' to express this recurring urge, and in this chapter I relate it to how it shaped the future of the farmers, who were anxious beings, uneasy about their unknown future on the farm. I extend this anxiety to the entire white society that was oppressing a majority which they represented as potential criminals.

In chapter 4, 'Violence: The white farmers' fears erupt', I shift the focus of the problem, looking through the eyes of the state and the white farmers to understand how they rationalised violence on the farms. Through these eyes, there was no such thing as a human potato or brutal killings of farmworkers, only heightened sensationalism that served certain political interests intended to shift the Black people away from working on the farms. Thus, to these eyes the danger of the human potato was that it was disrupting the 'peaceful' social relations on the farms between white people and Black people, creating a state of social chaos.

I offer an overview of the state's politico-economic interventions in agriculture to show the anxiety of the white society. On the farm, white farmers shared the land with their Black dispossessed labourers. White farmers identified their being in the world with their attachment to the land, and the threat to their core selves was embodied in the Black worker, whose claim to that land they could exorcise only through violence. By criminalising the Black person through the petty offenders' scheme, the white farmer's plan was to prevent farm tenancy, thereby consolidating the land in the hands of the white farmer. The scheme provided him with workers who could not lay claim to the land. However, the problem was not completely solved, for the potatoes that looked like humans not only exposed the unjust social relations on the farm, where workers were buried in the planting fields, but also laid bare the haunted conscience of the farmer and his anxiety about his relationship to the land in the future.

In chapter 5, 'These eyes are looking for a home', I follow the lives of former labour tenants on the farms in Bethal. I draw on the transcripts of interviews conducted by Dr Tshepo Moloi from 2007 to 2008 to understand the history of Bethal and the violence that happened on the farms. In tracing the former labour tenants, who now reside in the township of eMzinoni, I investigate what it meant for them to grow up on the farm. Through this, I provide a sociological reading of dispossession by going beyond the white society's fears of the future projected in the negative ontological category of a Black person. I ask if a Black society exists. This question is sociological, since it aims to look at what constitutes society. I approach the sociological reading of dispossession in three ways in this chapter.

There is, firstly, the question of the identity ascribed to Black people, that negative ontological category of being a k____r, and what it meant in terms of the impossibility of forming a social collective on the farms. Because of this negative method of identification, the Black person suffered from trauma and demonstrated a desire to move away from this present.

Secondly, I focus on education. I argue that education was used not only to organise and institutionalise violence but also to rationalise it, to make violence a way of life for Black people. This education, grounded in violence, aimed to shape a future in which Black people on the farms always remained docile.

Thirdly, entwined with these two approaches, I relate the question of a society to the state, that entity in society that is an expression and protection of the identity of the members of society. Given that the segregationist and apartheid state did not recognise Black people as a collective belonging to a society, this left many farmworkers desirous of a state to protect their interests. I argue that the desire for a state is a desire for a future, a future where Black people can define themselves positively, a nascent desire for a collective definition. The state is always reflective of this nationalistic desire, and the apartheid state was precisely that – an entity that aimed to protect the anxieties of the white society by ensuring that it distinguished them from the 'inferior Black people'. However, the view here is not absolute or pessimistic in its casting of the problem, since I show that the labour tenants on the farm had a plan for shaping the future through making a home there. Even though the farm is violent, the tenants and their families looked beyond the violence and hoped for a better future. It was this hope that carried them every day.

With the assistance of Xender Ehlers, I visited the farms that were mentioned in the archival articles about violence-related cases. We went to farms located on the northern side of Bethal: the Legdaar farm, where Cornelius Mokgoko died; Schurvekop and Kalabasfontein, where there were cases of flogging of workers covered by the Reverend Michael Scott; and Blesbokspruit, the farm where we believe Henry Nxumalo might have worked to prepare his exposé for *Drum* magazine. At Blesbokspruit we discovered a compound, and one of the labour tenants confirmed that it used to house prison labourers. We also went to Roodebloem farm.

The aim of the visits, for me, was to see what the land looks like and what issues the labour tenants are currently facing in Bethal, the focus of chapter 6, 'Bethal today'. Through the eyes of the labour tenants, the argument is that just like the eyes of the dead yesterday, the eyes of the living today are still looking for a home on the South African farms. This is an eschatological search, for a place to be buried in, a place to rest in, a piece of land to be returned to. These visits helped me uncover the spiritual meaning of land beyond the violent ontological meaning of belonging, which is expressed through the idea of ownership of land. Through the eyes of these workers, we can see that just like those who died during the scandal of the discovery of the potato that looked like a human being, they are still looking for a home, despite the country's transition from its violent past to democracy. At the same time, this past is recalled and used to make claims to the land.

For the labour tenants, the present is still haunted. Through their stories we see that their eyes continue to search for an elusive home and that they are in a constant struggle to make a home in a land that does not belong to them. This haunted land reflects the ontological nowhereness that the violence of ownership today continues to enforce. The argument is that ownership is an instrumental way of concealing the spiritual question of land. To go beyond ontological nowhereness is to uncover the importance of the eschatological gaze through which the farmworkers look at the land – as a place where one day their spirits will rest but which presently remains a violent place, a haunted place, where there is no rest.

I conclude in chapter 7, 'Our eschatological future', by arguing that to work the land is to understand its secret. One day the body will be returned to this land. The land is our eschatological future. The scandal that resulted in the potato boycott of 1959 led to an exposé of not just the dead humans that came back looking like potatoes, but also the nature of their violent deaths. They were buried like dogs, as if they did not belong, and yet they used to work the land. A question may arise from the understanding that a contestation is a dispute involving two vocal parties. Why is this history presented as a contestation if the farmworkers were silent and did not fight the farmer? The mere presence of Black workers in large numbers on the farm was enough to create anxiety for the farmer. And the contradiction of the petty offenders' scheme was that it brought to the farm not just labourers but 'criminals', potatoes that did not belong. The juxtaposition is that in those times the threat came from the criminal, whereas in today's South Africa the threat comes from farmworkers who have rights, and from a state tasked with defending those rights. What we learn is that the way ownership is conceived always creates anxiety and this anxiety is always related to the unknown eschatological future – that the owners might lose the graves of their ancestors just like the landless. Therefore, violence is used first as an ontological claim (belonging) to secure a future home (for their dead bodies and those of their unborn). What remains unsolved in this story is the future of the Black farmworkers who are still facing violence and earning next to nothing. Where does the Black farmworker belong in this land?

Chapter 2 | Whose eyes are looking at history?

> Mrs Kgobadi carried a sick baby when the eviction took place ... Two days out the little one began to sink as the result of privation and exposure on the road ... its little soul was released from its earthly bonds ... They [Kgobadi family] had no right or title to the farm lands through which they trekked: they must keep to the public roads – the only places in the country open to the outcasts if they are possessed of a travelling permit. The deceased child had to be buried, but where, when, and how? This young wandering family decided to dig a grave under cover of the darkness of that night, when no one was looking, and in that crude manner the dead child was interred – and interred amid fear and trembling, as well as the throbs of a torturing anguish, in a stolen grave, lest the proprietor of the spot, or any of his servants, should surprise them in the act. — Solomon Plaatje[1]

The anguish of dispossession in South Africa is neither the untold truths nor the many spoken truths of how a family, in the place of their birth, ended up stealing a grave. The anguish comes from the eyes of the ones who had to steal the grave and bury their own in a hurry. As if that is not enough, the moment of dispossession is thought of today as part of a vile past that is no longer relevant to us.

The history of dispossession in South Africa should instead be seen as part of our historical present. Our history is forever present in our social order. To locate it, we need to look deeply into South Africa's vast hectares of land. What we might excavate will be ugly, but it will also reveal the deeper meaning of dispossession – that once people are removed from the land, not only do they become slaves, they also become 'criminals' whose entire existence is a journey to nowhere.

This is a condition of ontological nowhereness as exemplified in Solomon Plaatje's *Native Life in South Africa*, where he documents how the 1913 Land Act made criminals of all those Black people (labour tenants) who refused to abide by the law which stipulated that they would become servants of the farmer and work the land along with their cattle. Plaatje encountered families in Bloemhof, Transvaal, who had become criminals as a consequence of this resistance. These families had trekked into land unknown to them, risking capture and the charge of trespassing. They travelled with stock, and their ownership of that stock might be questioned. Many had thought that the law was applicable only in the Orange Free State and ignored warnings that it also applied in other parts of the Union of South Africa. All natives without land were turned into servants. Those who resisted were, in the words of Solomon Plaatje, 'wandering [to] somewhere'.

The Kgobadi family was one such group. Not only had they lost their cattle in the trek, but they had also lost their offspring in the cold night and had to steal a grave to bury their child. The Kgobadi family were staring at their future through the child's death, a future in which they did not know where they would die and be buried. This story of dispossession aptly expresses ontological nowhereness. Deep within the story is a revelation of how dispossession creates the burden of not belonging to the land, not having a place called home, being forced to make ends meet in the city and potentially being criminalised for not producing a pass.

When the dispossessed Kgobadi family looked at the vast landscape of South Africa, their eyes were looking into a past, the present and their future. It was a past snatched violently from them and a present that they refused to accept. The future was filled with hope that despite the loss in the past, there would surely be a place where they would make a home and would ultimately be buried. If they did not keep moving, they too would be without a grave. If they had no hope for the future, they could easily have returned to their past in the Orange Free State, to an environment they were familiar with – yet they continued to trek, losing possessions, losing life, losing their future through the death of their livestock and their offspring. Who knows what promises they made as they interred their seed?

The Kgobadi family were also looking at the land with an eschatological gaze. This was a spiritual look at the land, which they saw as the first and last destiny for their spirit. To create a home and be buried in the land is a spiritual activity. This eschatological gaze was not limited to how the dispossessed saw their fate. In Bethal, when people looked at the potatoes and said, 'These potatoes look like humans', theirs was an eschatological gaze. The statement is not coming from a person betrayed by their eye who ends up seeing the impossible, but is about an eye that already sees the truth in what is perceived – a human potato.

Here I am mapping the eye as a prejudiced organ and bringing forth a puzzle. The conundrum lies in the difficulty of appreciating the story of dispossession when the eye is an organ of prejudice. The question of whose eyes are looking at history becomes important if we are to ascertain the meaning of the history of dispossession. I follow the eyes of the people who no longer had a home in the country of their birth to understand the meaning of this uncertainty and their relationship with this new state of existence. I invite the reader to look at dispossession with me, through the discredited eye, the eye of the dispossessed one, who steals a grave, who works the land, who is killed in this land and is then concealed. In so doing, I take a different look at the nature of farming in South Africa and its potential to create jobs, to boost the economy and to feed the nation, whose turbulence in recent times is seen as resulting from a decline in employment and is exacerbated by white farm killings and the calls for expropriation without compensation. In my PhD thesis I argued against the narrow view of seeing the land through an economic lens.[2] In that narrow view, the farm killings and the debate of expropriation without compensation are linked together – because they build into the economic view of the land question. The expropriation without compensation is seen as condoning the killing of farmers and killing farmers will destroy the agricultural economy. This reduces the land question to an economic question without looking at questions of belonging to the land.

Today our eyes must appropriate the look that is given to the land by those who have been discredited. Through these eyes, we will conclude that our present is steeped in a past that entailed death in the making of the South African farm, and we will see what dispossession is and how it relates to the future and our current temporality. Our eyes will meet other eyes also looking at the land: the eyes of the white farmer and the European settler, who came to legislate the theft of land and normalise the violence of dispossession under law. Violence and law became part-ners to ameliorate the anxiety about the future felt by the minority gov-erning the land. The law rationalised the discrediting of land ownership by Black people by recognising that the minority were justified owners because they were adept at large-scale farming.

To show how this history of death and dispossession is revealed in the present (beyond the focus of Bethal and in conversation with Bethal), I look first through the eyes of a sangoma (a traditional healer or diviner) in eMsinga, KwaZulu-Natal, to focus on the demand made by the dead whose graves were concealed for many years on Glenroy farm, Dududu. This is the first eye, the spiritual or the eschatological eye, which relates to death and to the demand of the dead for freedom. The biopolitical power[3] of the state is insufficient to explain what happened to those who died at Glenroy farm and the forensic eye is brought in to 'freeze time' with the aim of giving a scientific (chronological and genealogical) account – yet this eye still cannot give a material account of the past.

The narrative then shifts to the past, to the prison cells in Fordsburg, Johannesburg, in 1949, two years after P.J. de Beer, the Native Commis-sioner, piloted what became the notorious petty offenders' scheme. In this prison I look at the history of dispossession through the eyes of De Beer and how he argued that farm work was good for the prisoners (this despite rumours that farmers were murdering their workers). The paternalism of the commissioner was shared by white liberals, who believed that there were ways of improving the farmworkers' working conditions and that they were not equally bad on all farms. This eye ignores the nature of dispossession in South Africa and its making of ontological nowhereness.

Another set of eyes is those of the farmers in Bethal who felt that the state did not understand their position. These eyes saw the critical articles in the press by the Reverend Michael Scott and others, and claimed that such sensationalism showed no understanding of what was good for the natives working on the farms. For the farmers, the issue was that the workers were prison labourers or criminals and were always trying to escape from the farms. For the farmers, the reported deaths of workers were a distortion of what was happening on the farms.

After looking through these eyes, I return to why the eye is crucial when revisiting the history of dispossession. The eye of the farmer is the eye of authority on the farm; the eye of the farm labourer sees the farm as ontological nowhereness; the eye of the state includes the forensic eye that freezes time; the spiritual eye can see the spirits of the dead. In theorising the history of dispossession, we must see not only with the material or physical eye but also with the spiritual eye. The case of the Kgobadi family, for example, requires the spiritual eye to see the theft of the grave as an act that signals the coming future for the dispossessed. This future shapes the relations that Black people are to have with the land and gives a new meaning to the land that was dispossessed; as criminals, the dispossessed will not be returned to the land and their death will not be a spiritual passing to the other world to be welcomed by their ancestors. The death of the dispossessed was meaningless, their future futureless, since they did not belong to the land. In living and in death, the dispossessed were turned into wanderers seeking freedom, but they were chasing an unreachable horizon as they did not belong to the land. That is why the apparitions of the dispossessed demanded to be freed when they appeared in Gogo Mshanelo's visions.

To see with a spiritual eye

In 2015, Gogo Bongekile Nonhlanhla 'Mshanelo' Nkomo, a sangoma from eMsinga, detailed how, in the previous year, she was haunted in her visions and her sleep by ghosts demanding to be set free 'as you have freed others'[4] or to have their spirits released.[5] In isiZulu this is called 'ukuboniswa', a spiritual moment when ancestors bring visions to the sight of the diviner. These visions relate to the present or the future. Thus, ukuboniswa is to see with a spiritual eye. In her visions, Gogo Mshanelo would see scores of people without limbs or who were burned, stretching their arms towards her and demanding their freedom. She tried ignoring their calls but they began to manifest through her body, tormenting her to the point where she became sick, had unexplained bruises and lost her teeth. Who were these people who were so vicious in their demand for freedom? The response was that they were souls 'wandering, searching for peace and freedom'.[6] Gogo Mshanelo would later discover that the bodies she had seen were buried on Glenroy farm in Dududu, on the south coast of KwaZulu-Natal and now owned by Illovo Sugar (eMsinga, where Gogo Mshanelo is from, is approximately 250 kilometres away from Dududu). The sangoma tried to alert the government; she went to the MEC's office to relay this encounter with spectres, but to no avail.

With the assistance of a chaplain from Pietermaritzburg, together with her initiate and a friend, she visited Glenroy farm and asked for permission to see the gravesite, claiming that she had a relative buried there. 'She was taken to a burial site, but she insisted it was not the one she had seen in her dreams. She was eventually led to the site she had seen in the dreams.'[7] Her traditional healer colleagues later advised her to approach the provincial Department of Arts and Culture and the matter was handled by the MEC, Ntombikayise Sibhidla-Saphetha. In March 2015, it was reported that 100 dead bodies were discovered, buried on that farm.[8] This discovery led the MEC to call for the documentation of 'the untold stories of KZN's history'. The suspicion was that the bodies were those of prison labourers transported from Umzinto, near Newcastle, to Dududu. The owner of the farm had died in 1985 and the farm was sold around that time. The community attested to the farmer being an evil man known for torturing and killing prison labourers on the farm between the late 1950s and the early 1980s. Therefore, the bones were likely to belong to prison labourers sent to work on the farm through the petty offenders' scheme. Those buried on the farm were classified as criminals.

Willie Ndlovu, who worked on Glenroy farm and resides in the area, indicated that those who worked on the farm 'were buried like dogs … there are many prisoners who died there. Once a prisoner had died, the workers would just dig a hole and bury them in an unmarked grave. We called the place where they were buried ezintandaneni [the place of orphans].'[9] This name is appropriate because those who died there were treated – and buried – as if they did not belong or have parents, but also because many of them left orphans behind. The pain of being buried like a dog is one that many prison labourers feared. They were reminded of the brutality of being homeless, of not belonging.

What we are discovering through these unmarked graves is that when we look at the case of Bethal and, now, the discovery of Dududu, burying people on the land and concealing their graves was not a rare phenomenon. In the archive of Bethal materials, we also uncover how the dead were accounted for once the farmer had killed them. Timothy Moloke wrote of the plight of his four friends who, when the farmer discovered that they were paid-up members of the SAIRR, were chased from one farm in the Belfast area to go work for the same farmer in Bethal:

[T]heir master or farmer's chief idea of ordering them to go to Bethal is to kill them by means of his plan because since he has known that they are members of the organisation [SAIRR], he is more against them.

The way in which he does when he wants to kill an African, they say, is … [h]e digs up a hole in his cornfield and takes his victim gently to it and orders him to get into it and then shoot at him and fills the hole with the sand goes to his local authorities and tells that the person left his farm without letting him know.[10]

It seems that on the farms in Bethal the time-honoured tradition was to conceal the violated dead bodies by burying them in the fields. '[M]any cases are concealed by means of burying the bodies of those who have been flogged and giving out that they have run away from the compound.'[11] These matters were brought before the courts and those who committed these atrocious acts were to be prosecuted. However, the spectres of Dududu remind us of the inadequacy of the language of legality to account for those who were landless, homeless and nameless, and tortured in body and soul. The officials in Dududu were digging up the past but needed tools to understand whether the dead were indeed victims of an unjust past. The eye of Gogo Mshanelo was doubted because it was a spiritual eye that saw the spirits of the dead before any evidence had surfaced. Through Gogo Mshanelo, we learn that the eye is an organ that can see things not only in the physical state but in the spiritual state as well.

What kind of freedom is demanded by the dead, so much so that in their death they can still extend their arms to the living? The problem is clear to see: dispossession as a condition of denying Black people freedom also means that even in death they will not rest peacefully.

Some sceptics viewed Gogo Mshanelo's visions or her ability to see the dead through a spiritual eye as chicanery because on the day of the visits to Glenroy with the MEC, she was wearing ANC regalia.[12] To them, this suggested that her eye was driven by her political views. But what about her body? Were they suggesting that the torture she suffered was self-inflicted?

The aim of looking through the eye of Gogo Mshanelo is to show that dispossession entails a spiritual problem and the demand for freedom by the dead. During apartheid, the land that the prisoners worked on was to lead to their deaths, but at the same time there was hope that their spirits would be freed. In the current period of our democracy, the dead return, demanding freedom, demonstrating that freedom has not yet been attained.

To see with the frozen forensic eye

The eye of Gogo Mshanelo was not enough. On 14 March 2015, the state requested forensic expert David Klatzow to aid them in making the past speak truth and justice. Klatzow indicated that 'the scene – and the wider area around it [the farm] will now need to be sealed off and frozen in time. There must be no disturbance of it with a front-loader or shovel … It must be excavated as one would an archaeological site.'[13]

This site of archaeological interest, frozen in time, was to speak about unknown injustices of the past. The ghosts (for the sangoma) and the bones (for the forensic expert) were to speak of their condition and allow us, in the present, to understand the past. The name of the sangoma, Mshanelo, which translates as 'broom', is significant, for as a broom she had the ability, which was recognised by the dead, to sweep below and even beyond what could be seen. The unearthing power of the broom allows it to go beneath the surface and reveal things we have forgotten – or never imagined existed. Gogo Mshanelo could not only sweep and reveal. She could also allow the wandering spirits to receive their freedom and find some solace. For the forensic expert, the bones were an archival source that spoke of the violence inflicted on the dead before they could finally rest and find their freedom. The problem was that these dead bodies were nameless and faceless, and it was difficult to find and notify their families. The burden fell on the living members of the families (if located) to come and claim their deceased with the assistance of forensics.

In a sense, this archive in the form of spectres spoke for itself. Using the body of the sangoma as a medium, the ghosts' discontent and pain, and the violence against them, could be personified, made manifest through her body. The ghosts demanded freedom and could not be ignored until the bodies were excavated. Unfortunately, the process of excavation may have served the purpose of archiving, which encourages the remembrance of the dead only for those dead to be forgotten once again. The bones revealed the horror in the history of South African farms, but with apparently no follow-up undertaken, the case seems to have gone nowhere.[14]

As we move to the farming fields in Bethal, we should see the story in this small town in Mpumalanga not as an aberration but as forming part of the story of dispossession that rendered many Black people homeless, nameless, faceless and graveless.

To see with the eye of the state

When the matter of farmers killing workers in Bethal was revealed in the media, there was a need to understand how such a system had come about. The SAIRR carried out an investigation of the Native Commissioner's office in Fordsburg to ascertain whether P.J. de Beer, the Native Commissioner, was coercing the natives to work on the farms.

The subsequent report was written by Frederick van Wyk, assistant director at the SAIRR, as the main author; William Ngakane, who served as a fieldworker, was the second author:

> Mr de Beer, who has been in the employment of the Department of Native Affairs for approximately 45 years and who has been at Fordsburg for 7 years, knows the Africans very well and seems to be highly respected by them. Those Africans who know him well – and there are many – call him 'Oom Piet' [Uncle Piet]. His whole attitude towards the Africans is very friendly and sympathetic, and both Mr. Ngakane and I were impressed by the friendly atmosphere which prevails in the hall in which he usually addresses the Africans.[15]

The report conveys a different account of how prison labourers worked on the farms. Eyes such as Van Wyk's would never find anything amiss in what De Beer was saying because it confirmed his belief in the need for a white person to look after the Black person. Let us hear the voice of De Beer as he speaks to the prisoners housed at Fordsburg, linking himself to them because he was also born on a farm:

> I have come to talk to you, not as an official but as one of your own ... In my young days I was never taught not to play with you and I was frequently naughty with you. My father always said 'The Africans are our people'. We (you and my father's people) were never poor. We had our land and our cattle. You and I know that life, but we cannot live that life in Johannesburg. We cannot keep cattle, and life is expensive here. What you should do is to go to places where you can work and save money. Here in Johannesburg you earn money and spend it all immediately. Here you never save money.
>
> Now I want to offer those of you who have no work and no passes an opportunity to work in our biggest national factory, by which I mean the farms, the factories which your fathers and my fathers built and where you and I grew up. You can learn more today on the farms than before and become skilled workers as drivers of tractors or workers on threshing machines. If you can drive a tractor you are a full-fledged driver of practically every vehicle and will obtain a licence which is valid in any part of the country. In addition, you will get comparatively high wages. In order to live you must learn different kinds of work. It is experience that counts. I don't want to discourage you but you must remember that machinery is fast ousting you for employment. I know of work previously done by 500 Native boys. The same work is now done by one machine and 8 boys. But you need not suffer as we have our own factories turning out goods which we cannot import owing to import restrictions. So we are building our own factories and in two or three years' time I am sure you will be able to choose your own employment. With the money which you can now save, you

should also be able to build your own factories. The Government will help you, if you save the money. We should not stay in town merely because of the bioscope ...

A man walking about Johannesburg is no good to anybody. You must remember the law which we call Section 29 (Act 25, 1945) applies to black and white alike. The Africans who won't work at all are sent to Leeuwkop [jail] and the Europeans to Swartfontein [jail]. We also have men who won't work amongst white people. If we do not work we walk about idly, get into mischief and eventually even cut other people's throats.

The conditions on the farms are good and our Union Africans never run away from them. It is the extra Union Africans who run away. I think you are all good enough for our farms.

You have now heard what I said and I thank you for listening to me. I now leave it to you to decide what is in your best interests.[16]

This time travel through the eye of De Beer is an effort to evoke in the minds of the prisoners memories of those days when natives were happy on the farm and had cattle. De Beer is calling to mind a different side of dispossession: in the present state, the prisoners desire those long-gone days when they had land and cattle, but life in the city will not earn them that. This search for happiness as described by De Beer could also present itself to the prisoners as a question: where will we die? This question made many detest the farm, for they had to work the land without belonging to it. De Beer's vision was that in the past the native had been happy, and a glorified past could be realised again in the future if the prisoners went to work on the farms as prison labourers.

De Beer did not know that the happiness that existed in the past, now stolen by the present, could not exist again in the coming future. The renewal and rehabilitation project De Beer spoke of as a project of justice – namely, to escape a prison cell – was to backfire. Those prison labourers came back as ghosts of those buried on unknown farms – as in the case of the spectres from Dududu – possibly violently killed, demanding freedom from the present future. De Beer treats the present as if the present is not the future of the past; as if in that past and in that state of happiness those who found themselves in prison cells were not running away from the happiness that he thinks existed on the farms. In this he deflates the horror on the farms by laying the desertion from them on those he sees as 'extra Union Africans', meaning immigrants who worked on the farms. The conditions on the farms were as horrendous for the prison labourers as they were for the immigrants. It was those conditions that forced many to run away – or to want to run away.

To see with the paternalistic eye of the white liberal

During the period of media coverage of farm killings in Bethal, a letter was addressed to Frederick van Wyk by a Mrs A. Hoedemaker (from Bathurst in the Eastern Cape) in which she expressed her concern about how other farmers treated farmworkers as labourers. She indicated that she was trying to find ways to help the farmworkers she had employed to deal with social, economic and health problems.[17] She stated that she had tried to secure the services of a social worker, but the cost would be 20 pounds per month, which she could not afford. She was concerned about the state of being of the workers:

> Surely the Bantoe [sic] WERE a happy people, but don't you think, they have lost a lot of their natural happiness in the last years? More in the towns than on the farms, I think but even here: is there not a bitterness in the young people's hearts, when they see, how the old ones get old? Not in all of them, but some seem fanatic.[18]

The eyes of Hoedemaker see bitterness. She is concerned and her letter to Van Wyk is intended to find solutions. She wrote that she 'do[es] not look on them as labour but as people of South Africa'. This line impressed Van Wyk, whose response was that such an attitude

is a good starting point and if only your attitude could be generally accepted by South African farmers, farm labourers would, I am
sure, benefit very greatly. I do think that the most important thing
is that farmers should treat their labourers with courtesy, consid-
eration and kindness and then the other things will follow natu-
rally. At the same time, one must always bear in mind that these
people are, generally speaking, very conservative, their views of
what is important in life often differ very much from our own and I
personally do not believe that we should aim at drastic changes and
drastic reforms, provided our attitude to them is one of kindness
and fairness. From a European point of view I think it is true to
say that they are, generally speaking, backward, both educationally
and in their way of living, but I am of the opinion if they are well
housed, well fed and sympathetically treated, they are very happy
people, something which, I am afraid, cannot always be said about
the highly civilized and the well-to-do. Because they are backward
they are not always able to grasp the full significance of reforms
aimed at their own improvement and my experience has been
that they often regard attempts to improve their conditions with
the utmost suspicion and sometimes even with amusement at the
peculiarities of the Europeans. One is, therefore, really forced to
move slowly, the ideal being that reforms should take place without their being aware of them. This calls for the utmost patience
and understanding and a willingness to carry on in spite of the
lack of appreciation on their part. So often their attitude is one of
UZUNGADINWA NANGOMSO (Please do not tire to-morrow)
i.e. (Please continue giving us gifts, etc.) ...[19]

Van Wyk's language is as paternalistic as De Beer's. They were alike,
both born and raised on the farm side by side with Black people. They
perceived themselves as benign spirits interested in the development
of the backward native. Van Wyk was of the view that reforms should
happen slowly. Mrs Hoedemaker was dealing with an ungrateful bunch

who always wanted gifts. This language seeks to show how backward Black people are and that the burden of the white nation in South Africa is to modernise them and assist them. This is an expert speaking here (also speaking on behalf of the knowledge gained by his friends), for he 'grew up on a farm – in the Eastern Cape – and lived there for fourteen years, I have now lost touch with farm life. However, I shall try to give you the outline of a plan which I base on my knowledge of Xhosa farm labourers ...'[20]

This eye was a prejudiced eye, which formed part of the society of white liberals who believed they had the best interests of the native at heart since they knew how the native behaved. It was a metaphysical eye, the view of those who believed that their actions were based on sound ethics, for the good of the lazy native. This eye reveals the meta-physics of representation.[21] In recognising their shared history with the dispossessed, they also misrecognise the people in front of them and suspect that their unhappiness might be based on their ungrateful-ness or laziness. The solution: continue to send them to the farms, but improve their working and living conditions. When confronted by the evidence that workers were dying on the farms, they claimed that only a few farmers were bad, not seeing the violence on the farms as part of the nature of South African agriculture and that the dispossessed were unhappy because they were dealing with the condition of ontological nowhereness.

The eye of the state and the farmer in Bethal

The media coverage of violent abuse in Bethal sparked a social furore. The Minister of Justice, H.G. Lawrence, gathered farmers in the area in July 1947, and at this meeting the farmers and government expressed how they saw the problems. The minister claimed that the problem was not one of violence but that, although the prison labour system ensured a supply of labour, workers deserted the farms because they were criminals. The farm was a route to their freedom and a means to avoid serving their sentences.[22]

To the farmers, there was nothing wrong with what was happening in Bethal. One of the farmers at the gathering before the minister was open about the issue:

> The matter had got so bad that farmers did not trouble any more to report cases to the police. (Applause.) After all, if a farmer was lucky enough to catch natives who had deserted and who had cost him a lot of money, there was provocation for him to give them a cuff (klap). (Applause.) He was not condoning ill-treatment or certain serious assaults, however.[23]

A bit of violence should be permitted because the farmers were dealing with a childlike criminal who needed their supervision and guidance. The farmers did not believe their problem needed any investigation for the solution was clear: when dealing with desertion, a tougher hand was required. Mr Lawrence said that while he agreed that there was a need for control where many natives were employed, 'it was illegal for anyone to deprive another person of his elementary rights of freedom. In no circumstances could farmers lock up their natives or keep guards over them when they went to and from their work.' He reassured them that they should '[f]orget Mr. SCOTT. Forget that gogga. Don't let one man be such a spook to you.'[24]

Reverend Scott had been invited to attend a meeting in the Bethal town hall, where the farming community showed him how they felt about him:

> As Mr Scott rose to speak shouts and boos came from every part of the crowded hall. One man rose and appealed to the meeting to allow Mr Scott to speak, 'Do not be afraid, let him speak, we can fix him later,' he shouted.
>
> 'We won't let him,' shouted the crowd. 'Let him go to his coolies.'

Mr Smit [president of the Bethal branch of the Agricultural Union, who chaired the meeting] assured the audience that Mr Scott had promised not to be long, and pleaded with them to let him have his say. 'Not a word,' shouted the crowd.

A suggestion was made that the meeting should vote on whether Mr Scott should be allowed to speak. A man in the crowd called out: 'Let him speak in Afrikaans or not at all.'

'If he can't speak in Afrikaans let him speak in K____r,' called another voice, and another added a few moments later: 'Or in coolie.'[25]

Scott eventually spoke, but he was hardly heard because of the howling from the crowd.

He never did manage to reach his conclusion ... that dairy cows were far better protected by law in terms of living space and sustenance than were compound labourers. Before this insight could be imparted, the meeting had effectively been taken over by an Afrikaner woman in the audience who virulently insisted Scott had insulted Afrikaner motherhood, her own three sons, and the entire nation ...[26]

Scott was condemned as someone who had insulted the entire white nation; he was a troublemaker, a spook, a communist. Such insults are interesting for they reveal the eye of power and how it perceived what was written about Bethal, even though there was evidence that farmers in Bethal were violent and were killing their workers. The entire white farming community in Bethal saw the scandal as an externalisation of their internal problems, an intervention into how things were on the farm. They continued to argue that their problem was that they were faced with natives who ran away from the farms and therefore they did not commit any murder. The natives who were unaccounted for were reported to have simply run away. In Scott's report he had indicated that most deaths on the farms were the result of indunas (foremen) or farmers beating people to death for trying to escape, as had been the case with Franz Marie and Phillip Lebovo in 1944. Regarding the cases of 1947, Mr B.H. Wooler in the Bethel magistrate's court stated:

> Europeans because they were better educated should set an example. Instead many continually had sjamboks with them: if they carried sjamboks they get into the habit of using them and when they lost their tempers they used them indiscriminately and without justice, they punished excessively and without care and the time might come when such punishment would lead to loss of life and to the most serious consequences for the assailant.[27]

To the judge, violence was the way of life for the farmers; it was how they solved the problems on their farms. The unjust usage of the sjambok was the law on the farm – and justified. This violence was again revealed in 1959 at the inquest of Cornelius Mokgoko, whose death sparked the potato boycott.[28] Cornelius had arrived on Legdaar farm on 2 March 1959 and died there three days later. (Legdaar was one of the farms I visited during my fieldwork.) His body was exhumed on 19 July 1959 by the Bethal magistrate for an inquest to determine whether he was a victim of violence on the farm. At the inquest, Simon Skosana took the stand as a witness. He said Cornelius was 'thrashed every day by the Boss boy because he was slow'. The boss-boy shouted at him: 'When an animal does not work we throw him out – this is Bethal.' The workers were seen as animals, and if they were slow, beatings would make them improve. Cornelius was beaten over the head and body with a stick. Blood was coming out of his mouth and ears. The 'white boss of the farm' also joined in the beatings when he was told how lazy Cornelius was. Despite his wounds, Cornelius was forced to continue working, denied water and shade, 'and died on the ground where the other workers could see him'.[29] The death of Cornelius was to be an example to other workers: in Bethal, if you do not work, you die.

Yet his body did not rest in peace, for it was to be subjected to the biopolitical power of the state through an inquest. Skosana's account of how the man had died was validated by the exhumed body, the wounds serving as evidence of the violence. Through Cornelius, we see how the farmers saw those workers who were not used to farm work; they saw such workers as needing a sjambok.

Interestingly, the death of Cornelius made the activists in the country see Bethal differently. They saw the area as needing political action; this led to the boycott of the potatoes from this region to pressurise the farmers into treating their workers justly.

Theorising from the eye

The question of whose eyes are looking at the history of dispossession is about the pace and order of this world that one tries to theorise. To theorise from the eyes is to bring the question of representation differently – not from the issue of enunciation,[30] but from two important stances: the ethical and the eschatological. The eye is an ethical organ for it sees and recognises the face of the Other. In this seeing and recognition, it may also misrecognise, and we have seen that the eye of those in power is involved in this act of misrecognition. This misrecognition is premised on the position one occupies, and therefore the eye is also an organ that is socialised to see in a certain way.

From the eye of a liberal white minority, De Beer and Van Wyk had been socialised to see a Black person as forever in need of white aid. No matter how ill-informed they might be, no one could shift their views because they had grown up with Black people and therefore knew them. From the argument that this was how things were on the farm, the liberals were comforted by their altruism and the farmers by their brutality. However, both eyes misrecognised and misrepresented the plight of the dispossessed who were working the land.

On the other side, we have encountered the eye of the Black person who was dispossessed of the land and whose plight was represented spiritually; the fact of not belonging to the land meant that the dispossessed had no place to call home, and therefore no place to die. In meeting Gogo Mshanelo and learning of her visions, we see through her eyes the continued horror suffered by the dispossessed. In her case, the dead sought freedom from the farms as they were killed and buried like dogs in unmarked graves.

As beautiful as farming is, it also conceals the terrible conditions that the dispossessed have suffered. That is why the eyes of the white minority erupt with fear when they see Black people working the land. As a minority, they cannot fully trust their state of being. This conflict is ever-present in agriculture and it is mediated through violence.

Chapter 3 | Bethal, the house of God

When Jacob awoke from his sleep, he thought, 'Surely the Lord is in
this place, and I was not aware of it.' He was afraid and said, 'How
awesome is this place! This is none other than the house of God; this
is the gate of heaven.' — Genesis 28:16–17[1]

The history of Bethal can be traced back to a donation of land made
by two farmers, Cornelius Michiel du Plooij and Petrus Johannes
Naudé, who intended to create a small town to serve the needs of the
isolated farmers in the area. They named it after their wives, Elizabeth
(Beth) du Plooij and Alida Naudé. Farming in Bethal relied on labour-
intensive crops such as wheat, rye, maize and potatoes.

The private town was demarcated in 1868 in the south-eastern part
of the farm Blesbokspruit. To the early settlers (Voortrekkers) in desperate need of a place for safe residence after they had been pushed out
of Natal by the British occupation in 1843, the small town was seen as
a holy place – they dubbed it 'the abode of God', after Bethel in Jacob's
dream in the book of Genesis. George Hudson, colonial secretary at the
time, published the proclamation of Bethal on 23 February 1898, making the town 'subject to the administration, control and management of
the Government of the Transvaal'.[2]

Making a home and working in hell

The Bethal magisterial district incorporated the farms in the Standerton,
Middelburg and Ermelo districts, with a surface area of 1 270 square

miles and a total district population of 750 adult white men.[3] There are no readily available demographic data for white women – and there is no mention of Black people existing in this area before the settlement of the white population, except as labourers. As whites settled in this district in the first half of the 1800s, they needed labour, and this led to an increase of Black people in the area.[4]

During the Anglo-Boer War, Bethal was destroyed (see figure 3.1). On 20 May 1901, Boer women and children and Black labourers were driven from their houses to the outskirts of the town in open wagons, and the next day the town was set alight by the British soldiers. The townspeople watched as Bethal burned for two days, after which they were taken to concentration camps. This was all part of the scorched-earth policy of the British to prevent the Boer commandos from obtaining food and information from Afrikaners.[5] The situation was similar across the Transvaal. The Boers surrendered at Vereeniging on 31 May 1902. As a result of their protracted suffering, many Afrikaners swore that they would not mourn again and that they would not be separated from the platteland.[6] Separation from the land always created an anxiety within the Afrikaners, and this anxiety was always related to the future, to the prevention of usurpers (whether British or Black) taking what the Afrikaners regarded as theirs.

In the 1920s, large-scale farmers were experimenting with methods of increasing efficiency. These included the use of labour tenants on farms, the employment of contract workers, the recruitment of foreign workers from across the borders – in the main from Nyasaland (Malawi), Mozambique and Rhodesia (Zimbabwe) – the compound labour system and, later, the use of prison labourers.

The eastern highveld is a water-rich area compared to the rest of South Africa and highly suitable for agriculture. The soil to the north and east of Bethal is most suited to potato planting. Today potato production has drastically declined in the area. The only farm in the district where potatoes are still being produced lies just east of Bethal, near the hamlet of Davel.

1901 — Ruïnen van de Kerk te Bethal.

Figure 3.1: A photograph of a church in Bethal in ruins after the Anglo-Boer War. (National Archives and Records Service of South Africa)

From the 1920s, to exploit the richness of the area, the farmers began to experiment with systems like those used in the mining industry, such as housing workers in compounds and binding them to strict contracts. The area also saw the implementation of the ticket system, which stipulated that workers had to work for 30 days a month. The wages varied. By the 1940s, the set monthly wage for prisoners was nine shillings. What the ticket represented was the idea of 'no work, no pay'. This modernisation was driven by farmers such as Israel Lazarus, one of the largest maize producers in the world at that time. (In '1924–1930, the average yield for the Bethal district was 9.24 bags per morgen and for the "maize triangle" was 6.35 bags per morgen. Lazarus used about twelve hundred tons of fertilizer a year and maintained two thousand oxen.')[7] The farmers in this region were described as very rational and enterprising, as they simplified tasks using methods similar to the

Taylorist[8] model with the emphasis on piecework. The workers were divided into gangs that performed certain tasks and were paid using the ticket method to prevent absenteeism.[9]

The people who occupied the land in Bethal from around 1910 included immigrants from England and Lithuanian Jewish immigrants such as Israel Lazarus. In Bethal they were comforted, for in their father's house there were many rooms.[10] These rooms were heavenly for some but hellish for those who came from Nyasaland or Rhodesia and for the 'criminals' who worked the land. It was this hell that put the Bethal, the house of God, on the front pages of newspapers. When one looks at this hell with a biblical eye, it is as if the parable of the rich man and Lazarus was turned upside down in the house of God. Now Lazarus was in hell working hard to ensure that those in heaven were comfortable; or maybe the hell was on this earth for the rich man who had named the land the house of God, for he knew that one day he might not be in the bosom of Abraham. Perhaps these wealthy farmers' constant anxiety was that 'it is easier for a camel to go through the eye of a needle than for someone who is rich to enter the kingdom of God'.[11]

During her time as a labour reporter, Ruth First observed and reported on violence perpetrated by white farmers on Black workers in what was then the Eastern Transvaal, and recorded her findings in the 'Bethal Case-Book'.[12] The violent treatment of Black workers in the region was attributed to the shortage of labour on South African farms, which led to the introduction of the petty offenders' scheme as a measure to solve the problem. First shows how the geographical positioning of Bethal made it difficult for farmers to attain labour power:

> Bethal is plumb in the centre of the Transvaal farming area furthest from any African Reserve. The Free State draws seasonal labour from Basutoland, and the squatter system is extensive; Natal's wattle and sugar plantations are close to Zululand; the Transvaal citrus areas in the north of the province are fed their labour from the great trust areas in that vicinity, the Western Transvaal borders

on Bechuanaland. But for Bethal's maize, wheat and potato lands there is no ready-to-hand source of labour.[13]

In 1947 the Reverend Michael Scott, with the help of Henry Nxumalo (who in 1952 published a follow-up story on Bethal in *Drum* magazine), discovered farmworker conditions that left them aghast. Black people who were coerced to serve their prison sentences in Bethal were stripped naked and given potato sacks to wear so that they could not run away from the farm. Among them were children as well as workers on the contract system who were known as 'ama joint' (those who had joined). The natural assumption would be that inside a potato sack there would be potatoes. Instead there were humans. This was the living human potato labouring in the fields, not the one that turned up in Johannesburg resembling the dead human potatoes who were violently killed. In her 'Bethal Case-Book', First depicts the life of farmworkers: enduring hours of back-breaking work, digging up potatoes from the ground with their hands, living in conditions unfit for human beings and being terrorised by the 'sjambok-carrying farm "boss-boys"' (see figure 3.2).[14]

The prison labour system First describes had existed in the past through various schemes. The petty offenders' scheme of 1954 was an attempt to solve the problem of labour shortage on the farms. It is apparent from the archive and the findings by Scott that the harsh conditions in Bethal did not begin in 1954 when the scheme became official. They had been covered in the press as far back as 1929, when a farmer had flogged a worker to death, pouring scalding water into his mouth when he cried for water. The conditions in Bethal were so appalling that they led Scott to argue that slavery was 'more humane than a system which ignores the fact that a man is a man, not such so much that he is a man with any political or religious rights, for that is a very far cry from the present situation on many South African [farms] ...'[15]

Like Reverend Scott, those who read the Bible looked at the land in Bethal with moral eyes. Farmers reading their Bibles were conscious of

Figure 3.2: A team of workers being monitored by a boss-boy on a horse, Bethal, 1952. (Photo by Jürgen Schadeberg from the Schadeberg Collection)

the reality that 'owning land' in the Union of South Africa meant that they had acquired it through subjugation and that their success was linked to the violent treatment of the Black farmworkers. It is these eyes that led Scott to provide in his report a detailed account of the conditions in the Bethal compounds. He reminded his readers of the hypocrisy: 'reading their Bibles by the light of their fires as they watched over their womenfolk, their children and cattle, to guard them from marauding beasts, and the indigenous populations. Perhaps they hardly distinguished between the two.'[16]

Today it is difficult to say *autres temps autres moeurs* (other time, other customs) because those times and those customs continued into the twentieth century. Martin Murray shows that the behaviour of capitalist farmers (and the recruitment system of 1910–1940) continued to reflect the belief that the natives 'were not thought of as sharing an identical human nature, a common economic rationality, and a similar psychological outlook with their European labor. Born of an inferior race, they were best suited for certain types of manual labor.'[17]

Bethal was a holy place indeed, for the Lord had granted to the 'superior beings' (who had subdued the land and all the beasts that came with it) fertile soil and 800 millimetres of rain a year. Bethal was consistently praised for its contribution to commercial agriculture in the Union – in the 1940s, the town accounted for about 60 per cent of the country's maize output. It was also promoted as a peaceful holiday resort for those seeking to get away from city life.[18]

In such a place, there was a need for the law to govern the rooms of their father's house, and whites like Reverend Scott – as one farmer commented – could not be trusted for they were not authorised to be in the house of God. They did not understand the being of a native. This was a view expressed in the public meeting held in Bethal on 21 July 1947 and attended by the Minister of Justice, H.G. Lawrence, to discuss the implications of the brouhaha caused by the release of Scott's 'Memorandum on Compound Labour Conditions in Agriculture, Bethal District'. The *Rand Daily Mail* quoted a Mr Lotter, who spoke at the meeting:

The likes of the Rev. Michael Scott come in here unauthorised and entice *our natives* away to get them to Orlando [Soweto] … he eats and lives with natives. Is that a decent European? (Laughter and loud applause and trampling) [emphasis added].[19]

The laughter and applause were not merely a revelation of the farmers' denial. They exposed the fact that when it came to their labourers, the farmers did not believe they were dealing with human beings who deserved justice or equality. Bethal was not a home for Black people, no matter how long they laboured on the land. "'Bethal,'" said one African, "is the worst place that God has made on earth."[20]

There was no peaceful sleep for Black people and their children who had to work the land. The potato that came back looking like a human was to remind South Africa of untold terror, past and present.

There is no going back home

The labour regime on the farms and the contract system drew on the ontological insecurity and nowhereness of Black people in South Africa. Simultaneously, the contract system was part of the efforts to 'modernise' agriculture and an instrument of stability. Natives were to be encouraged to be interested in farm work, and the contract was confirmation that they had consented to fulfil their duties. The contract – which the farmers were obliged to offer – stipulated the duties, the wage earned and the rations to be received. It was intended to circumvent arbitrary rules laid down by the farmer – that is to say, to take away from the farmers the idea that they were the law.[21]

The Department of Native Affairs was one of those institutions that encouraged the modernisation of agricultural labour relations and promoted the contract as one of the steps towards this. With the introduction of contracts, 'touching the pencil' became the equivalent of a signature. The action meant that the farm labourers who 'signed up' agreed with the terms of the contract even though its conditions were not read or explained to them. A large majority of the work seekers were illiterate, and many of those who touched the pencil complained that they were duped by recruitment officers who had told them they were going to work in a factory, not on a farm. The farmers knew about this. When the workers arrived on the farms, farmers were able to use the 'law' to manipulate them into following orders. The farmers reminded workers that they were on the farm because they had touched the pencil – that is, signed a contract. In his *Drum* exposé, Nxumalo noted witnessing that several labourers had 'touched the pencil' just to get a job.[22]

In this case, the word 'contract' can be seen for what it was: a con, or deceit, regarding a tract of land. The language of legality was used to bind workers to the farm, even though signatures were illegally obtained. Each party to a contract is supposed to read or be read the contract and consent that they have understood what was written there and agreed to its terms.

The contract served only to help conceal the terror of going to work on the farms around Bethal. The town was well known as a horrific place for workers to find themselves in, so much so that labour recruiters and farmers recruiting on the border of Rhodesia would change the number plates on their vehicles so that the workers were not aware that they were going to the Eastern Transvaal. In his undercover assignment for *Drum*, Nxumalo learned that, in fact, none of the workers understood the contract or knew the details of the work they would be doing, or even how long they would be on the farm. However, the desperation and the long search for a job made countless workers fall into this trap. As soon as one touched the pencil, there was no going back home. One worker told Nxumalo:

> I had been looking for work for two months in the city of Pretoria when I met this white man. He asked me if I wanted work. I said Yes. Any type? I again said Yes. He told me that he knew of a bass who wanted boys to work on his lorry that carried produce between the market at Johannesburg and Pretoria ... I found the baas. He told me that he did not have any more work for lorry-boys, but he had work on his farm and in his mine. I had to choose between

those two. I did not take long; for after you walk the streets for nine weeks you are glad for any work. I told him I would work for him on the farm …

I was sent to the yard behind where I found six other men: four Nyasa and two Basothos. We spent three days there, and were not allowed to go out, for the baas said we would be leaving at any moment. On the fourth day we were marched to the office of [Native Commissioner] Motlhe. We were marched into an office, and after some writing by the white men we were told to hold a pen in the hand. After we had all done this, we were told that we had signed a contract for six months' work on this white man's farm. This alarmed us and we three Basothos asked to be cancelled. The baas said we could rub our signatures off with money only. We had no money, so we also climbed into the canvas-covered lorry with the Nyasas. We climbed into this van on a Saturday morning in January of 1949, in Church Street, and climbed out of it with cramped legs that night in Leslie [near Bethal]. We were led into a compound surrounded by a high stone wall, given a blanket each, and told to sleep in one of the low, dirty, mud-walled long rooms by a black foreman.[23]

The prison labourers also confirmed that they did not wish to be in Bethal because many of their friends had died and if they complained, they were 'going to be killed'. The national organiser of the Penal Reform League of South Africa, citing the report by William Barney Ngakane on farm prisons, noted that the prisoners were not given a 'free choice' to go to work on the farms:

It should be the *free choice of the prisoner*, and it has been pointed out that in quite a number of cases at the Fort, relatives of prisoners have arrived in good time to pay fines, only to find that the prisoners had already been despatched to farms as private labourers. In some cases the prisoners had been recalled at the insistence of their European employers, but no Native would probably have sufficient knowledge or power to demand this re-call as a legal right [emphasis added].[24]

The contract rested on the false assumption that those employed on the farms knew their rights. As will be seen, the usage of the 'law' by the farmers reflected neither their ignorance of it nor their paternal attitudes, but was instead a historical reading of the law, which saw it from the eyes of the dispossessor. The dispossessed were mere servants. In the eyes of the farmer, he *was* the law on his farm. The superintendent managing farmworkers knew that, on the farm, the white person was the law – or, to extend the argument,[25] in the Union of South Africa, the white person was the law. The contract was a method of binding workers indeterminately to the land.

In documenting the plight of those from Nyasaland, Scott noted that 'a single third class ticket for a Native male from Blantyre in Nyasaland to Johannesburg cost £3 1s 6d (females £3.5s) but a return ticket from the same place £7.13s'.[26] The wage that many earned on the farms would not cover the trip back home, thereby forcing them to stay on the farms for years and send money home with those who were able to return. In fact, the system was rigged to prevent workers from going back home. This was the quandary of the man from Nyasaland who 'wanted to go to Johannesburg but had no pass to travel, had no money to pay the poll tax and was told he might be put in prison or sent back to the farms'.[27] There was no going back home. There was no home. This is the ontological nowhereness of those who worked and were bound to the farm.

A case that shocked the *Drum* offices was that of a man who went to Bethal in good health and came back home a few months later looking like an old man. He later died of tuberculosis.[28] Migrants hoped to return home with gifts and be able to make improvements to their homestead. This was a dream they would not attain. On the farms they became broken people, and if they did manage to return, they were not the same. If they ran away from the white father on the farm, they risked being confronted by the state demanding proof of where they belonged (the use of the apartheid pass) – and if they had no proof, they were sent to prison, then back to the farm. An example cited in *Drum* photographer Jürgen Schadeberg's memoir, *The Way I See It*, is a typical one:

> In 1950 Casbert Tuje, from the Cape Province, together with three friends, was recruited by the Siz' Abafane Agency in Natal and sent to a farm in Bethal to work as labourers for £3 a month. On Christmas Day they were invited to a party by a family who were living on the neighbour's farm. The farmer would not grant them permission to attend, so they left the compound without leave. When they returned to the farm the next morning, the farmer punished them severely by beating them. Then he handed them over to the police. They were brought before the court on a charge of desertion, and each was sentenced to two months. The farmer arranged that their imprisonment be served on his farm, where they were again thrashed by the 'boss boy'. Casbert sustained serious internal injuries and ended up spending several months in hospital.[29]

Nevertheless, leaving the farm became the objective of many farmworkers. The farmers were aware of this and it caused them anxiety. To the farmer, workers wanted to leave because they could earn better wages in the cities. However, through the typescript of the Native Economic Commission (NEC) of 1930–1932, Marian Lacey shows that farm labourers 'did not leave [the farm] simply because they were after better wages and conditions in town as most farmers claimed'.[30] It was the violence experienced under the laws favouring farmers that led workers to leave the farms. These laws were based on the paternalistic view that the farmers were the owners of the farms and they could do as they pleased with their labourers. According to Lacey, workers' reasons for leaving the farms were not economic. Drawing from the same typescript, she cites comments from the African Residential Association in Benoni to demonstrate how farmers used various ways to bind people to the farm:

The rule of the 'Bass' is so arbitrary and merciless that he sometimes imprisons them for imaginary offences even for petty mis-
understandings ... To say that natives come in Towns, in order to
obtain money for purchase of cattle for lobola is, to say the least,
untrue. In fact the disabilities under which the natives are suffering
are so many and varied.[31]

On the farm, full-time labour tenants were the core workforce. They
were born either on the farm's land or on surrounding land. They com-
prised families of four to eight people and they lived on the farm. In
exchange, they rendered their labour to the farmer. Failure to do so
would lead to their expulsion from the farm. They worked for three
to six months, depending on the agreement. They had a long history
with the land, and some could count their great-grandfathers as having
lived in part of the area they occupied.[32] It is notable that this group
were not strangers to this land and had not been duped into being there.
This was their home – but they had no claim over it. Their access to the
land depended on their labour power, drawing mostly from their children (see figure 3.3). But the capacity of these families was not enough
for large-scale farming; hence the need for farmers to draw on other
sources of labour.

Division of labour
Upon arrival in Bethal, Black workers were categorised as full-time
workers (mostly the labour tenants), prison labourers, and seasonal
workers (migrants) with contracts of up to five years. The immigrants
were recruited mainly from Nyasaland, Mozambique and Rhodesia.
First explains how they were recruited:

In 1946, just before the Scott exposures, there were some 40,000
foreign labourers contracted to farms in the Bethal district, the
majority from Nyasaland and the Rhodesias ... illegal immigrants
from across the Limpopo were screened at Messina and then again

Figure 3.3: Children working the fields, Bethal, 1952. (Photo by Jürgen Schadeberg from the Schadeberg Collection)

at Bethal, at a depot just outside the town, and given the choice between signing on for work on a farm or mine, or being deported back across the border.[33]

These contract workers were the 'ama joint'. They were also victims of the pencil-touching ruse. Ama joint was a preferred category for farmers because many native-born South Africans were said to be leaving farms for better pay on the mines. Regardless of the contract, however, farmers found other ways of keeping the labourers bound to the soil: workers could be accused of breaking a plough, for example, and made to pay for it, or they were in debt to the farmer for foodstuffs (such as tea, bread, sugar and tobacco) they had bought from the farm shop. Sometimes, to avoid being indebted to the farmer (who also sold clothes on the farm), the workers would clothe themselves in potato sacks. All of this reflected the difficulties of recruiting and retaining labour on the farms.

To ease these difficulties, prisoners – mainly those sentenced under the petty offenders' scheme – were brought in as short-term labourers. Under the overall supervision of the Department of Justice, the prisoners were housed in a prison built by the farmer. They were paid a wage of 9d per diem for the portion of the sentence they served and were given food. These workers mostly worked for 30 days, including Sundays, but excluding rainy days. Once released, the prisoner 'is for all practical purposes free, and need not, therefore, be medically examined when he is brought back to the gaol by the farmer after the expiration of his sentence to collect his wages and to be formally discharged'.[34]

Interestingly, it was by bringing in the prison labourers that the farm violence came to be exposed. The farmers' complaining about not having enough farmworkers to work the land and getting the state involved through the petty offenders' scheme eventually led to revelations about the dark side of South African agriculture.

Because farming in this region was labour-intensive, there was a need to ensure constant supervision, and this came in the form of 'baas (boss) boys'. These were men who were either workers from the local community or migrant labourers from Limpopo, Orange Free State, Natal and other parts of the Union.[35] They were the favourites of the boss; they were indunas (chiefs or overseers), to use the language of the mines. They made sure that the work teams were on the field on time and, given strict orders to deal with laziness, were to punish those who 'slacked off'. In court, they were seen as an extension of the white farm owner. On the farms, they were seen as despicable people because the boss-boys subjected Black people to violence on behalf of the white boss. The workers referred to them as 'aboMavukuvuku' (scumbags).[36]

The circle of authority also included the foreman/manager, who was sometimes present in the field with the sjambok-carrying boss-boy. Depending on the number of farms the farmer had, a white man might be employed to oversee the running of the farm and he would be the foreman. In the absence of the farmer, the foreman acted as the manager and the boss-boy carried out the rules and laws. However, some farmers did not have a foreman and opted for the boss-boy to be their right-hand man. The typical setup on the farm would be the farm owner/manager, who resided on the farm with his family, and the Black workers in compounds. Once the petty offenders' scheme came into effect, farmers erected prison compounds on their farms, where prisoners slept. These compounds were looked after by a superintendent who ensured the enforcement of law and order, often through the sjambok. The superintendent was in alliance with the farm owner/manager, and if the superintendent was not on the field, the boss-boy performed the task of ensuring that the prisoners worked and did not escape. The method was to administer lashes to any worker who slacked off or refused to work even if they said they were exhausted (see figure 3.4).

Through the eyes of Henry Nxumalo, 'Mr Drum'

When the story of the human potato surfaced and the violent killings in Bethal were receiving press coverage, followed by the potato boycott, the authorities were on alert. They could not understand what was happening in this small town. They wondered if the rumours of violence and the dead coming back as potatoes were true. In 1959, the Minister of Bantu Administration and Development, M.D.C. de Wet Nel, determined that there should be an investigation to deal with the allegations and that this investigation should speak to the victims as well. The purpose of the investigation was 'for the sake of the good name of the farmers'.[37] The hope that those who were being or had been abused would talk was something that existed outside of those times. Workers knew full well that speaking against the farmer was like speaking against God. Addressing parliament, De Wet Nel used the language of paternalism, suggesting that the farm was a family unit with the farmer being the father and head of the family.[38] He eschewed the allegations of violence, arguing that farmers' wives were kind people who knew the families of the natives and took good care of them. The situation on the farms

Figure 3.4: Farmworkers – mostly children – being monitored by a boss-boy, Bethal, 1952. (Photo by Jürgen Schadeberg from the Schadeberg Collection)

therefore needed to be treated delicately. On the farm, workers dared not contradict God, the white farmer, and so their silence meant consent. Nxumalo described the situation:

> One day the police came to the farm. We were taken together before them, and they asked us if we were satisfied with the conditions. For a moment nobody answered ... then some said 'Yebo, Nkosi.' My heart was filled with anger at this untruth; but I knew why they had said it. They hoped to curry favour with the white men. Nobody could dare to contradict [them] ...[39]

That was why Reverend Scott required the assistance of Nxumalo and why the SAIRR required the assistance of Ngakane – so that the workers could see a black face and feel comfortable enough to pour their hearts out. Workers knew that they could not speak to a white person about their working and living conditions. They did not see them as individuals but rather as members of the oppressive white society. The question of race also affected how the truth was spoken and to whom it was spoken. Many workers told Nxumalo that they also feared speaking to the police.

Nxumalo not only exposed that which was not visible to many eyes; he also interpreted the pain felt by those who had no viable channel to voice their grievances. The eyes of Nxumalo become the eyes of the worker, not only because he saw the workers but also because he worked the land in Bethal alongside those who were afraid to speak against the farmer. At the same time, Nxumalo aimed to make the labourers' plight visible to people who were not on the farm, mostly white liberal activists and institutions that were driven by the need for justice for the farmworkers in Bethal.

Several newspaper clippings on farm violence collected by Nxumalo may help set the scene and solidify the idea that events in the 1950s were merely a continuation of that which had begun a long time before:

1929: a farmer in Bethal ... was found guilty of tying a labourer by his feet from a tree and flogging him to death, pouring scalding water into his mouth when he cried for water.

1944: a labourer in Bethal was beaten to death for attempting to escape ...

1947: a farmer assaulted two labourers, set his dog on them, flogged them and chained them together for the night.

1947: a farm foreman was found guilty of striking a labourer with a whip and setting his dog on him.

1947: a foreman was found guilty of ill-treating African labourers ...[40]

Judge J.R.A. Leibrandt also gave judgment on a number of assault charges. These included:

[1947:] Paul J. van der Merwe, aged 51, a farm foreman, and Jacob Mknwena, a boss boy, both of the farm Zaaiwater, were found guilty of common assault ... [2] Hermanus van Niekerk, aged 55, foreman of the farm Rietviel [charged] of common assault ... [3] Matthys Stufnus Ackerman, a foreman of the farm Zondagsfontein, was found guilty of common assault ...[41]

And in 1959, a farmer named G.S. Lourens was found guilty of assaulting convict labourers. He was sentenced to a fine of £50 (or four months' imprisonment), with a further two months' imprisonment being conditionally suspended for three years.[42]

Such revelations were a public scandal, and the SAIRR, through its field officer, Mr Ngakane, tried to ascertain whether the allegations by Nxumalo were true. This resulted in his producing the 'Report of Inquiry into the Working Conditions of Prison Farm Labourers'.[43] While the investigation was in process, on 15 March 1954, Ngakane sent the letter that set me on my course of investigation (see Prologue) to Henri-Philippe Junod, the national organiser of the Penal Reform League of

South Africa, in order to corroborate the seriousness of Nxumalo's findings that were published in *Drum*.

Looking through the eyes of Nxumalo, it becomes clear that his interest was to show what was hidden on South African farms by focusing on the social relations between the farmer and workers. He also wanted to understand why the workers did not leave the farm. While working in Bethal he discovered a 'prologue to hell': after eating meat, those who worked the land would be thrashed and forced to work. Meat was a rarity; workers ate mielie meal with skimmed milk or potatoes. If they ate meat, they would be woken up in the morning by the 'baas boy' who would say in Sesotho, 'Le jele nama ea kalajane, kajeno le tla e patella' (You have eaten the meat of a cheat and today you will pay for it).

In June 1952, the same year as that of the Bethal exposé, *Drum* published another of Nxumalo's investigative stories: this time into the 'tot system' (or 'dop system'), where farmworkers, living in poor housing conditions, were paid with alcohol.[44] The increased consumption of alcohol, and diseases like tuberculosis, were causes of early deaths. The tot system was condemned by Nxumalo, who argued that the state should do away with this form of payment instead of allowing it to exist in the Transvaal. In February 1953, he investigated the sugar farms in Durban and found that the low wages farmworkers earned there forced them to borrow money from the farmer, who then used this to his advantage by drawing up a contract that would bind them to work for him for longer.[45] This was a vicious cycle. Many workers were in debt to farmers for more than 10 years.

In March 1955, three years after his story on Bethal broke, Nxumalo returned to the subject of farm violence when he worked at the Snyman farm Harmonie near Rustenburg. Wearing torn clothes and walking to the farm on foot so that he would be more likely to be granted a job, he was hired and promised a wage of £4 a month (which was later raised to £5) and a monthly ration of mielie meal. In this story, Nxumalo's interest was to discover whether the violence on the farm had subsided after the owner, Johan Snyman, had been arrested in 1954 for killing a prison labourer, Elias Mpikwa. During the trial Snyman was quoted as saying, 'If he [the native] does not know how to work, I will hit him for a week until he knows.'[46]According to the evidence presented in court, Mpikwa was beaten by Mr Snyman and his son with the assistance of an African foreman (boss-boy) named Jantjie Thlome.

While covering the above story, Nxumalo was also following three other stories reported in the South African press about the violent treatment of prison labourers on Western Transvaal farms, especially in the area of Koster. As in Bethal, workers on these farms also slept on sacks, wore sacks and used sacks as 'plates' to eat on. Nxumalo's purpose this time was to find out whether a farmer being punished by the law would result in the cessation of violent treatment of his workers. It did not take him long to discover that this was not the case. An encounter with the law did not stop the farm from being a place of violence. While working for Snyman, Nxumalo was overcome with exhaustion. When Snyman junior found him trying to catch his breath he tore up his pass and said, 'Now you haven't got a pass ... you can't leave without my permission: I can have you arrested and imprisoned. If you don't want to work fast like the others, I'll hand you over to the police and have you charged with refusing to work.'[47] Once this threat was voiced, the violence followed, but the farmer maintained that he 'treated his workers well and paid them well ... he clapped me on the left cheek with his open right hand, and told me to face the wall. Then he kicked me between the legs three times with his hard boot ... Then he told me he wouldn't stand any nonsense from me on his farm.'[48]

The labourers told Nxumalo that he was lucky that he got a beating because if Snyman senior had been present he would have undressed him and forced him to wear sacks so that he did not run away. Oh, the lowly potato sack. Who knew that wearing one would be one of the ways to prevent desertion? Wearing a sack was in itself a stigma, and if a farm-worker did manage to run away, whoever took that person on their land knew they would be dealing with a rabble-rouser, a cheeky k____r!

Nxumalo's conclusion was that nothing had changed on that farm, nor on many others:

> ... there are still many other farms like Harmonie. Unless workers are given freedom to complain or given leave, and until convicts cease being sent to farms without supervision, there will always be cases of labourers being seriously ill-treated. Not only farmers, but African foremen and labourers take part in these brutal assaults. Mr. Drum ... appeals to the authorities to take steps to end this dreadful barbarism, *which has done such untold harm to race-relations* [emphasis added].[49]

The clear indication was that violence against workers was not only happening in Bethal but was widespread over various farms in the country. But because workers could not speak out against the farmers, it was difficult to see their struggles. Nxumalo made an appeal to the authorities to intervene in order to thwart the barbarism on the farms that was doing 'untold harm to race-relations'. Interestingly, as we look through the eyes of Nxumalo, we recognise that he is preoccupied with the issue of race relations. Was it not the case that, at this point in time, South African race relations were already ruined and the situation on farms was indicative of that? At the same time, this issue of race is related to the issue of a voice. In reading the archive, it is difficult to find a voice of farmworkers speaking directly or collectively of the brutality they endured. One way in which workers reflected this violence, however, was through the names they gave to certain individual farmers, examples of which can be found in the archive: Madubula (the one who shoots); Manyenye (earthquakes); KwaMbawula (the fire); uMabhulala Umuntu (the one who killed a person), which was a name given to Snyman; and Jy Moet (you must). The names were a way of alerting fellow labourers to what they were dealing with in the hope that they could avoid the tempestuous side of the farmer; alternatively, the names were given to warn those seeking work to enter at their own risk.

It was also believed that the spirits of the dead remained on the farms. In the story of Snyman's farm, one labourer, a cook known as Picanin, claimed to have seen the ghost of Mpikwa 'sitting on the box in the shanty where we have our food'. This issue of the spirit was understood by workers as seen through Picanin's eyes: a body has a spirit, and once the body is killed, the spirit does not disappear from the farm. It continues to be present where the body perished. In a case such as this, a name given to the farmer might also indicate that the spirits of those he had killed continued to follow him and the farm was a haunted place. If one fails to see the spirit, one needs only to note the names given to the farmers to understand the magnitude of that which needed to be unearthed.

Violence and the future

My grandmother would use a particular Zulu word, 'iqunga' (the urge to kill), when explaining that once a person has killed or has taken part in a violent event, the conscience of that person will be burdened by the spirit of the dead. No matter how hard the person may try to conceal it, the only options available are to kill again, to go mad or to speak the truth. They may also consult an inyanga (traditional healer) for intelezi (traditional medicine) to get rid of the spirits.

Weren't all these farm killings – and not only the ones that were reported – a product of that which could not be located in that present state, a product of a conscience that was haunted? Derrida wrote that a haunted conscience 'is not only haunted by this or that ghost ... but by the spectre of the truth which has been thus repressed. The truth is spectral, and this is its part of truth which is irreducible by explanation.'[50] Those farmers who killed did not confess; they were forced to speak the truth in a court of law, where the violated native was supposed to gain justice. This justice did not to speak to the problem, however. The farmer kept the land and returned to his home. We do not know what burdened the conscience of the farmer or of the land. The ultimate violence experienced by those who were dispossessed was their deaths;

they were prevented from being returned to the land in the way prescribed by Black customs and tradition.

To the farmer, to employ violence was to secure the future, to ensure that the living, and even the dead, did not have a claim to the land. One reason why farmers chose to recruit labourers from other countries is that workers who were not from the Union could be told to go back home; they had no claim to the future of the land. They were subjected to the same violence, however, as the other workers.

To Nxumalo, race relations were at stake on the farm. According to my postulation, it was the future of the land that was at stake. Many of those who worked the land through the land tenure system were born on the farm and could count their ancestors as occupying the land. This was the unspoken contestation. As the study on Transvaal farm labour conducted by Edith Rheinallt Jones in 1945 was at pains to show, the relationship between land and labour is one which is shaped by dispossession, and the native's refusal to work on the farm cannot be divorced from how they responded to their detachment from the land. Rheinallt Jones cites one labour tenant who said:

'... my grandfather woke one morning at his own kraal and found a white man who said "You are living on my farm and you must work for me."' Such families have now with changing ownership, with sub-division, with more intense cultivation, little real security unless they make themselves good and diligent farm workers. Even when they have been in town ... and worked faithfully and well for periods, they dislike long days of farm work for anything but very short periods. 'The farmer expects us to work from sunrise to sunset. We have to go out and work even if it is raining.'[51]

Through the land tenure system, the dispossessed were forced to work the land they and their ancestors had occupied, and if they did not, they were chased away. They could easily be rendered homeless. What if one day in the future they decided to claim this land as home? The violence was a reminder to everyone who was Black and who laboured on this land that this was *not* their home. This, perhaps, was the silence that was punished, the silence that was dangerous, for we have not heard voices of resistance emerging through a collective movement by the living dead for the dead. On a farm the whites were a minority, living far from the city life and from access to police and the military. Therefore, the violence they inflicted was intended to thwart a future violent revolt by the Black people, to keep them docile, to prevent them from contesting the land.

Addressing the violent nature of South African dispossession on farms is crucial. It speaks to the entire capitalist system that demanded cheap labour on farms, and it was fuelled by the racism that rendered all Black people in South Africa as criminals. This resulted in South African prisons becoming overcrowded, which in turn prompted farmers to build prisons in their farming districts or on their farms, supposedly to 'ameliorate' the conditions. For example, in 1967 it was found:

> Of the more than two million crimes reported every year in this country of only 17.5 million persons, nearly one-third are not crimes in the ordinary sense but crimes that only a black man commits by being in the wrong place, with the wrong papers, at the wrong time. It is unlikely that there is any people in the world among whom a prison record is more commonplace than it is among Africans.[52]

The farmers and the state, in relying on the prison labour system, were aware that the system reflected the ontological nowhereness of Black people. Bethal spoke directly to the systemic issues that reflected the anxiety of white society. In dealing with violence, we are dealing with a question of the future. When we do not know what we do not know – when we address only that which we know – the future will always escape us. Karl Marx reminds us that the capitalist is always oriented towards the future, which is built in the now through the exploitation of the labourers, which must continue again tomorrow. In 'The Modern Theory of Colonisation', Marx speaks of a separation of humans from the means of production as a condition carried by the capitalist to other countries so that what began in the mother country can carry on in the future. Marx stated: '[N]ever mind, national wealth is, once again, by its very nature, identical with misery of the people.'[53] To Marx, the capitalist future is always in crisis and a revolution is a product of a future that is always coming. That is why the capitalist is never at ease. The spectre of a revolution directed towards private property continually haunts them. The ghosts of Bethal and many other South African farms are yet to speak.

Ghosts may haunt the perpetrators, but justice may not come because the perpetrators may keep the crimes a secret, even though they are living a tormented life. However, truth remains spectral. A case in point is the death of Henry Nxumalo. When Nxumalo was killed in 1956, Leonard Mlotshwa, who was 22 years old, appeared in court in 1958 and it was said that he had confessed to killing Nxumalo. He argued that he only confessed under the advice of Victor Dube, who said that if he confessed, 'he would be taken away from the farm where he was being forced to work and where, he said, conditions were unbearable.'[54] Remember that Nxumalo was against prison labour. Was this revenge from the ghost of Nxumalo? South Africa remains haunted by its past. Revisiting Bethal is a reminder of the truth that is yet to be spoken by a haunted conscience. The ravages of this truth remain ever grand in the vast hectares of land in South Africa, which are sealed and protected as 'private property'.

Chapter 4 | Violence: The white farmers' fears erupt

> A great historian who needs no introduction to some of us ... once
> said of our beloved continent – and I think with a certain amount
> of justice – that before the white man came there was no African
> history to speak of in this darkest of the Dark Continents ... African
> history commences with the arrival on African soil of the first white
> man. The history of Africa is the history not of black Africans but of
> white men in a foreign environment. — Lewis Nkosi[1]

The terror of white society

If one follows the thesis put forward in the epigraph by Ndi Sibiya's
white lecturer in Lewis Nkosi's 1983 novel *Mating Birds* – that African
history is about vulnerable white men who had to survive in an unknown territory – then the use of violence to protect oneself becomes
justifiable.

In South African history, the vulnerability of white society played
out as the 'native problem'. The native problem was not only about the
conquering of the unknown Other; it was also about the making of
social relations to ensure that the future of the white society would be
secure in this foreign land. This meant securing land and transforming
the native whose land was stolen into a docile labourer. Nowhere was
this so clear as on the farm, where the white farmer and his family created a home side by side with those who worked the land and who saw

the land they worked on as their home, and as the place where, after death, they would be laid to rest.

Although this book is written primarily through the eyes of the farmworkers, it is worth considering for a moment what the world looked like through the eyes of the white farmers who criminalised the workers, who saw them as non-human and akin to the potatoes they farmed, and who even killed them when their terror erupted into violence.

The question for this chapter revolves around the levels of violence that went beyond labour and racism into the heart of the meaning of 'owning' the land. To unravel this violence, I look at state intervention in the agricultural sector and how it was linked to the way white society perceived the Black person, as a labourer as well as a potential criminal. I offer an overview of the political-economic interventions in agriculture to show the anxiety of white society.

The petty offenders' scheme criminalised the native and prevented farm tenancy. This then consolidated the land in the hands of the white farmer by providing him with workers who could not lay claim to the land. However, the problem was not completely solved, for the potatoes that looked like humans not only exposed the unjust social relations on the farm, where workers were buried on the planting fields, but also revealed the haunted consciences of the farmers whose claim to land through violence concealed their anxiety. This anxiety was about their unknown relationship to the land in the future, when the land might be contested by those who worked it and also saw it as their home.

The coercive labour system and criminality

Many of those who seek to see the rationale of violence on the farms in Bethal want to place the focus on the state as arbiter of law and order. The coercive labour system is said to have been accelerated by three important interventions by the National Party: (1) the formation of the labour bureaus in 1951, in conjunction with laws that dealt with influx and efflux control; (2) the introduction of the prison labour system; and

(3) the creation of reaping times at harvest (which can be traced to the beginning of the Second World War).[2] The system of labour bureaus was not without contradictions, as the state classified Black people in the cities as tribalised or detribalised, arguing that industry should give first preference to the detribalised as they had permanent ties to the city, and not to the tribalised, who still had some links to the countryside. The policy makers saw the problem from a narrow economic standpoint. As Deborah Posel has argued:

> [They] treated the African labour market as if it were undifferen-
> tiated, disregarded workers' previous training and skills, employ-
> ers' prejudices and stereotypes as well as workers' own choices.
> Treating African workers as wholly interchangeable units of
> labour, the economic 'logic' of the Nationalists' influx control pro-
> gramme rested on the assumption that if the prevailing demand in
> any urban area was for x number of African workers, and the size
> of the local economically active population was x + n, then there
> was no good reason to bring more labour into the area until the
> growth in the size of the local demand exceeded n.[3]

Many of those who resided in the urban townships detested demeaning work and employers were forced to bypass the system and hire the tribalised. However, this was to the detriment of agriculture as it drew labour (the tribalised people) from the terrain of the farmers.[4]

On the other hand, there was the prison labour system, which also aimed to deal with the contradictions of labour recruitment and retention. Prison labour did not begin in the 1940s; the use of prison labour can be found in the early history of the Cape, when Jan van Riebeeck forced 'prisoners' to do public works, or later, in the nineteenth century, when prisoners were tasked with the building of roads. At the centre of the British Empire was the prison labour system, with the British East India Company being one of its biggest operators.[5] Therefore, to confront the prison labour system is to confront the question of how the colonisers dealt with labour scarcity and how to make those deemed 'lazy' work harder.

Prison labour has always been linked to physical punishment, a continuation of what had begun during the period of slavery in the Cape, when it was believed that to get the most productive outcome from the lazy, flogging was necessary. The prison labour system was premised on the existence of criminality in the urban area. Black people in the city were seen as potential labourers as well as potential criminals. The state deemed that to punish criminality, idle hands should be given work. To be a criminal was to refuse to comply – a form of resistance – or to ignore the law of the state. To farmers, criminality was their salvation from the problem of labour scarcity. A useful citizen rendered labour power to the labour market. Not to do so was to be a criminal, a potential threat of Black resistance that did not address itself to the civility of work. In this notion of criminality, there was no difference between a wallet snatcher and a political activist fighting for the rights of Black people – all Black people were considered dangerous. This was the notion of 'swart gevaar' (black danger), which called for white vigilance from the state (through policing) and affected interpersonal relations. In effect, every white person became a police officer to deal with the criminality of Black people, for merely by being a Black person one was a potential criminal – a saboteur, a rabble-rouser and a cheap, disposable labourer who belonged neither in the city nor on the farm, but only in the barren land called the 'reserves'.

Petty offenders' scheme: alliance of farmers and state

Ruth First has traced the genesis of the petty offenders' scheme as far back as 1932, when 'African short-term prisoners were contracted out as labour to farmers … [the scheme] was known as the "6d. a day scheme". Prisoners sent to prison for fewer than three months were handed over to farmers to serve their sentences on the farms.'[6] This scheme was compulsory. Consent of the prisoners was not obtained and they lost 'remission privileges which would have reduce[d] [the] sentence by one quarter if [they] remained in jail'.[7]

In 1947 the Native Commissioner's court in the area of Fordsburg, under P.J. de Beer, put forward a scheme whereby African men who were arrested for not complying with the Urban Areas Act of 1945 were not to be prosecuted but were to accept work on the farms instead. It would seem that De Beer made this announcement based on the interpretation of section 29 of the Act, which, he stated, applied 'to black and white alike. The Africans who won't work at all are sent to Leeuwkop [jail] and the Europeans to Swartfontein [jail]. We also have men who won't work amongst white people.'[8] The report on pass offenders by Van Wyk and Ngakane found that De Beer, and his partner Mr Morgan, saw themselves as playing a pivotal role in solving the labour problem on the farms and helping those natives who might find themselves in trouble with the law:

> They, therefore, felt it incumbent upon themselves to ensure the very best treatment for the Africans who go to the farms. Therefore, in front of the Africans and the farmers with whom employment is accepted they tell the Africans that if they have complaints these should be lodged with the farmer or local police. Quite frequently the farmers bring in employees with complaints which are then investigated. Mr. Ngakane feels that where a complaint is made to the police the probability is that the complainant's grievances will not be redressed because the police are members of the local community and will therefore avoid incurring the displeasure of the farmers.[9]

De Beer was said to be a friend of the native, not using force but showing compassion to those arrested. His case is interesting since it was discovered by the state that he had keys to one of the trucks that transported farmworkers, and the truck belonged to one of the farmers in Bethal.[10] The Department of Justice investigated the situation, and it was found that compulsion was used since a number of the petty offenders did not appear in court; it was suspected that they were sent straight to the trucks parked outside the Native Commissioner's office. De Beer had also threatened prisoners that if they did not take farm work, the ancestors would punish them. In this he used eschatological terror, invoking the spirits of their dead ancestors, to bind the workers to the farm. He was charged with corruption for using the past and the beliefs of the natives to compel them to work on the farms.

Despite several technicalities raised during this period, the scheme became extended in the General Circular No. 23 of 1954, in which the Secretary for Native Affairs, in conjunction with the Secretary of Justice and the Commissioner of the South African Police, indicated that this scheme was for the good of the natives as it would keep them from engaging in criminal activities. The petty offenders' scheme was presented as demonstrating the benevolence of the state, to save the native from becoming a criminal in the city. The crisis of overcrowding in the city was reflected in the prison system, where there was overcrowding in jails, and this resulted in farmers building prisons on their land to help ameliorate the crisis and offer an alternative – that of working on the 'national factory', the farm.

In the early 1950s, figures suggest a relentless drive behind the scheme: 40 553 prisoners were sent to work on farms in 1952, from a mere 25 000 to 30 000 in the years before.[11] And considering the participation of all 165 jails in the Union, it does not come as a shock that there was a sharp increase to 100 000 between 1953 and 1954, and an even steeper intake of 199 312 African men on farms between 1957 and 1958. Several farmers praised De Beer and the scheme because it seemed that the state was attending to their labour needs. The pace of state intervention in the agricultural sector can be seen in a letter written in February 1960 by V.R. Verster (Commissioner of Prisons) to the SAIRR research officer, detailing the number of labour prisons in the Union of South Africa:[12]

a) There are 24 farm gaols in the Union [these were built on farms] situated as follows:–

(i) 13 In the Cape Province at Soete Inval and Koelenhof, district Stellenbosch, Staart van Paardeberg, Simondium and Klein Drakenstein, district Paarl, Rawsonville, district Worcester, Obiqua, district Tulbagh, Dwarsrivier, district Wolseley, Riebeekkasteel, district Riebeek West, Warm De Doorns, Hawequa, district Wellington and Bien Donne.

(ii) 1 In the Orange Free State at Geneva, district Kroonstad.

(iii) 10 In the Transvaal at Leslie, Kinross, Trichardt, Ongesien and Geluk, district Bethal, Davel, district Ermelo, Hendrina, Woestalleen and Bulfontein, district Middelburg, and Driehoek, district Witbank.

Most of the prisons (13) were in the Cape. The Eastern Transvaal took the second spot. This need for labour on the growing number of prison farms led to *The Star* publishing an article, 'Scramble for Labour is Root Cause', on 13 March 1957, in which it was argued that the shortage of labour on South African farms was the cause of the violence reported on these farms. The article stated that the Transvaal Agricultural Union (TAU) had 'take[n] steps for closer liaison with the Native Affairs Department and the various labour bureaus to ensure that farmers get a larger share of available Native labour'.[13] From this, we also realise that farmers' unions like the TAU and the South African Agricultural Union (SAAU) influenced state intervention in agriculture. At the same time as the violence was occurring, they argued that this was not a common trend on farms, that there were only a few bad farmers, and that if they were found guilty, they should be punished by being delisted from the database. Yet Verster, in the above-cited letter, commented that the state was understaffed and could not monitor all the burgeoning prison farms. Thus, the farmers who were caught were either unlucky or were those closest to the Department of Justice, meaning that officials could easily access the farms. Given the South African terrain, it was difficult for an understaffed state to get to certain farms.

In a letter to the SAIRR, one Mrs M.L. Weston[14] put her finger on the problems regarding the petty offenders' scheme: that the farmers anticipated Black resistance to it (as indicated in the public gathering described in chapter 2). They worried that the prison labourers might escape, either from the farm or while being transported to the farm. Weston observed the behaviour of one farmer who developed good relations with a clerk in the police service who would get him more labourers than he required in case some escaped or decide to run away. Therefore, Weston concluded, this system of prison labour was 'manufacturing criminals'.[15]

Running away was in itself a criminal offence. This vicious cycle went from arrest to farm labour and then rearrest. It seems the connection between crime and farm labour reinforced the long-held perception of the farmers that even if some Black workers escaped from farms or preferred not to work on them, Black people in South Africa were *ipso facto* criminals. Thus, what the petty offenders' scheme did was to render violence as just, for the farmers were dealing with criminals – this in addition to the history that linked prison labour with physical force and slavery. This vicious cycle can be seen through the story of 15-year-old Moses from Alexandra:

Moses [was] returned on demand from a farm where he had been digging potatoes. He had still been at school, but was told that he was 15 and so should leave and apply for a pass. He was given a temporary document which he lost and as a result found himself arrested and taken to Court. According to Moses he was classified as juvenile and sent to 'S' Court, Johannesburg Magistrate Court where he waited all day without appearing and was then given four cuts and sent home. He walked to Alexandra. After a few days, during which he recovered from his cuts, Moses reported to the peri-urban authorities to try his luck again for a 'pass'. (He was too young for a reference book, apparently). The peri-urban official sent him home to get his sister to vouch that he was born in Alexandra, but before he could get his sister to the pass office he was visited in his home by a Non-European policeman. For the second time within a week Moses found himself in handcuffs and on his way to a police cell. At the police station a European police sergeant told him he was too young for farm labour and would have to go to 'S' Court again. A little later a Non-European police-man told him that the White sergeant was talking nonsense and that he had been 'sold' to a farmer. He never appeared in Court and protested that he did not want to go the farm. He was placed in an open-air 'cage' and eventually his name was called out. 'I told the White official (not a police man this time) that I did not want to go to the farm. But he said I must go. He did not tell me to which farm or which district or how much I would be paid. Later that day I was taken away with seven others under the guard of bossboys.[16]

The capitalist alliance: a period of gold-maize

South Africa's first and second industrialisation during the early decades of the twentieth century is described as a period of 'gold-maize' in which the state had to ensure that it not only attended to the needs of mining, but also supplied capitalist agriculture with cheap labour. In looking at this period, Archie Mafeje contended that the purported existence of an alliance between gold and maize suggests that there was a homo-geneity of interests between foreign capital, mostly in mining, and the struggling Afrikaners.[17] He argued that the Afrikaners were seeking to be the main benefactors of state policy and wanted to venture into other industries, therefore eliminating foreign capital. The only problem was that the Afrikaners did not have sufficient capital – that is also why it took them time to modernise agriculture – so they relied on their polit-ical power to ensure that they emerged as the dominant force.

This struggle is visible in the Bethal region, where the large-scale farmers who needed labour established agencies like the Transvaal

Farmers' Labour Agency, which acquired services from the companies that recruited in mining and began to recruit foreign migrants, who were mostly children, despite the state's disapproval of employing young boys. This form of recruitment was to encounter problems, since most of the countries that agencies recruited from had given the mining industry first preference. By the 1920s, the TAU was forced to complain about this bias. During this period the South African Party was removed from power. This was partly a result of the perception that the state was not caring sufficiently for the Afrikaners, especially the 'poor whites', which was exacerbated by the events of the Rand Revolt. These and other factors led to the election of J.B.M. Hertzog's Pact government, which emphasised the protection of the interests of white workers (especially the Afrikaners), and halted any recruitment in agriculture from other countries, favouring the employment of whites.[18] The big farmers in Bethal, such as Israel Lazarus, complained that the poor whites were 'too lazy to work' and 'what complicated matters was that farmers in the maize belt were located far from concentrated pockets of African settlement'. The entire Eastern Transvaal highveld was 'practically without Reserves'.[19] To deal with these challenges, the farmers pooled their resources through the recruitment agencies and lobbied the state. This view of the period locates violence from a perspective that aims to show the relationship between the state's interests and the capitalists' interest in agriculture. Thus, it sees violence as a rational attempt by the farmers to have their interests secured through the state, and because the National Party drew its base from the rural farmers, state interventions in the labour market aimed to appeal to agricultural class interests.[20]

The aggressive manner in which the different strategies were employed by the state to obtain farm labourers can be traced as far back as the Hertzog administration in 1924. Marian Lacey argues that Hertzog did his utmost to ensure not only that Black people did not have land (in dealing with the native question), but that they had little option other than to render their labour on the farms.[21] Thus she surmises that the reserves were always a threat to the farmers and an opportunity for the mining capitalists to attain cheaper labour. She shows how, through different platforms, farmers went on to disregard the creation of reserves and the problem of indirect rule that denied them labour. It was believed that if Black people had land they could return to, then they would not offer their labour power to farmers. Despite this rationalisation of violence, the question is: were there no other options available to the white society?

The farmworker as a potato

One simple answer to the question of why violence was used against Black people is that the native was not seen as a human being. Punishment and discipline were meted out merely to change their relationship with work. Thus, the native was seen as an idle being, a sack of potatoes.

After the release of Reverend Scott's 1947 report on agricultural labour in Bethal,[22] one reader of the *Rand Daily Mail* indicated that whites in South Africa showed no sympathy for labourers in Bethal:

> This comparative indifference (how different would have been the reaction were the roles of complainant and accused reversed) seems to be caused by the habit of regarding the natives not so much as fellow human beings entitled to sympathetic help in their upward climb, but as labour to be kept available for our profit.[23]

Within the debate of state intervention in South African agriculture there were those, like the SAIRR, who shared the above view, but who went only so far in terms of seeing the problem as negatively affecting race relations and how this would have important bearings on the future of the country. Henry Nxumalo shared the same sentiments in his *Drum* coverage of Bethal through his disclaimer that '[w]e are all too aware of the damage to good relations between the races that the conditions at Bethal have brought about, and we wish to do all we can to prevent such happenings in the future'.[24]

So, what was this future about? Why was this future secured by violence? Would treating those who worked the land as humans be enough?

For Ruth First, this future still related to securing labour for the benefit of white society. The scandal that was exposed in this period was that it was 'not an isolated evil' but brought 'to the fore some of the worst features of the apartheid cheap labour state and gives them a more hideous form'. Through this lens, the thesis is the problem of the labour shortage on South African farms. The antithesis is the fact that the farmworker system is violent and will not yield any form of development in South Africa since it restricts 'the farm worker from leaving one district for another in search of better work and high pay'. This antithesis expresses itself in the form of slavery described by First: 'The labourer is not owned bodily as were the slaves of old, but the wretched wage paid him for his back-breaking work barely distinguishes him from a slave, and he is no freer than a slave to leave the farm.' The synthesis is that in South Africa 'as anywhere else there is only one way to attract a flow of willing labour to the farms and that is to pay farm workers a living wage, to provide conditions fit for human beings and incentives to men to do farm work'. Despite citing the history of dispossession in South Africa, First does not go more deeply into the meaning of dispossession and why it took that particular form on South African farms. Rather, she asks why it is that 'the ambition of every son of every farm worker is to strike away from this misery to do better than his father did'.[25] To answer this, she says, we must consider the fact that Black people have no land:

> The Land Act of 1913 robbed him of all but 13 per cent of land; the poll tax forced him to leave his village to go [to] the mines or towns to earn a cash wage to be able to pay the tax collector; the Land Trust Acts threw squatters and labour tenants off farms without giving them any other home on the land. Over the years hundreds of thousands of families became wanderers, without land, homes or work in the countryside. From being the owners of their own fields and grazing lands they became hirelings and dispossessed servants of the new owners.[26]

Therefore, the National Party, with its desire to secure the interests of farmers, was 'plunging this country to disaster'.[27] For those who want to read the problem through the racial lens and through the rational capitalist logic of the state (responding to solve the labour crisis on farms), a question that might present itself naively, and yet is intended to defamiliarise the familiar, is: why would the farmers go as far as killing their labourers when they were complaining about labour shortages? An answer to this question debunks the rational logic of the capitalist state.

The smoking gun was said to be race relations in the countryside. This view was expressed in a memorandum issued by the SAIRR in 1959 and shared with the media and others who enquired about the farm labour question.[28] The memorandum called for government to intervene in the issue of violence on the farms since this was a matter of race relations. It noted that farm work was not appealing to Black workers and that such incidents of violence, as the TAU indicated, made it difficult to attain farmworkers. The conclusion for the union, which was also supported by the SAIRR, was the promotion of decent working conditions in agriculture (including better living conditions and higher wages). What is interesting about this material, especially the calls relating to decent work and a respect for the rights of Black workers, is that it draws on a discourse of rights; it acknowledges that even criminals have rights and that most of these rights were violated by the system under discussion. What is missed in this discourse is how the state itself – through what I read as systemic racism building on the ontological nowhereness of Black people – was able to create a condition in which being a Black person in the city was a crime if one did not produce the necessary documents that furnished one's domicile, employer's details or the person whom one is going to visit.

The law and violence: concealing the anxiety of the white society

The attaining of the criminal to work the land was not based on a separate event. The historical event of many Black people being uprooted from the land expressed itself in the cities with the rise of urban squatters in areas like 'Vrededorp, Newclare, and Sophiatown', with 60 000 people, and 'Alexandra Township (60,000), Western and Eastern Native Township (20,000) and Orlando (70,000)'. There was to be no family life or schools for those who worked in the European areas. 'Under these circumstances … [t]he moral sanctions and disciplines of tribal and family life are fast disappearing.'[29]

W.E.B. Du Bois argued that in the United States after the Civil War, it was normal for the white citizenry to express concerns about crime; they had never imagined that they would encounter a free Black man, and one can imagine encountering them in large numbers in a slum![30] All these people in the slums were like those who were squatting on South African farms. They were always suspected of being up to no good because they did not render their labour power to the whites. But such problems were seen as a problem of the irregularity of the law, rather than the result of the deeper issue needing to be addressed.

At the helm of showing that South Africa's legal system was filled with irregularities was the lawyer Joel Carlson, who brought forward several habeas corpus cases showing that many people ended up working on farms without their families being notified. The following cases appeared in the media:

a) By Innocent Langa for the return of his brother, Nelson Langa, from the farm of Mr. Hirschowitz in the Bethal district (July 1957);

b) By Dorkus Sadika for the return of her husband, James Musa Sadika, from the farm of P.J. Potgieter in the Heidelberg area (1959);

c) By Maria Mahloane for the return of her son Daniel from the farm of B. Feldt in the Kendal District (1959);

d) By Andrew Morgan for the return of his brother-in-law Paul Anthony from the farm of B. Feldt (1959);

e) By Mary Mtembu for the return of her husband Jackson from the farm of S.P. Botha (1959);

f) By Jackson Mtembu for the return of his friend Nelson Dube from the farm of S.P. Botha (1959);

g) By Usuman Adam for the return of his friend Samson Banda from the farm of S.P. Botha (1959);

h) By Violent Mamabola for the return of her son Andrew from the farm of S. Rubin in the Leslie District (1959);

i) By Esther Sonanzi for the return of her brother Alfred from the farm of S. Rubin (1959).[31]

Although still within the language of the law, Carlson's cases were popularised. This influenced the outlook of movements such as the African National Congress (ANC) regarding farm labour and added support for the 1959 potato boycott. The argument was made that many workers ended up on farms against their free will, even when they could prove that they had jobs. Yet it mattered not if they ended up on a farm unwillingly, for every Black person was a potential criminal, a fact those policemen in the city known as 'blackjacks' (because they were tough and highly prone to using violence) knew only too well. Thus, by framing dispossession using the language of rights and the law (the state), are we not merely prostrating to an idea of modernity and civility, and in so doing neglecting the nasty side of dispossession? One cannot touch the subject of law without speaking of violence. The law seeks not only to preserve 'law and order in society'; it also aims to have a monopoly on violence over certain individuals. If violence is not in the hands of the law, there is a threat to order in society, as well as a threat to the kind of society which the law, through the use of violence, seeks to preserve.[32] We can see that viewing the state and the law as rational apparatus has its blind spots: it gives too much credence to law and order being possible under a state that had already concluded, without any doubt, that Black people will forever be criminals. And therefore, as an extension of the state, the white society will always be suspicious of and anxious to rid itself of the criminal. This argument can be seen in Du Bois's contention that

> the South had no machinery, no adequate jails or reformatories; its police system was arranged to deal with blacks alone, and tacitly assumed that every white man was ipso facto a member of that police ... For, as I have said, the police system of the South was originally designed to keep track of all Negroes, not simply of criminals; and when the Negroes were freed and the whole South was convinced of the impossibility of free Negro labor, the first and almost universal device was to use the courts as a means of reenslaving the blacks. It was not then a question of crime, but rather one of color, that settled a man's conviction on almost any charge.[33]

Ivan Evans, in explaining the practice of lynching in his book *Cultures of Violence*,[34] which is a comparison of the North American South and South Africa, argues that southern American whites relied on lynching because they had no state; in South Africa this was not the case since there was a state that could make use of the law. Still within the logic of the rational state (law), Evans argues that another difference between the American South and South Africa is that after the Anglo-Boer War, the whites created a bureaucratic state that could manage Black people, and this was visible in how it dealt with the labour question. However, Evans does not deal with the fact that in South Africa the farm was an 'invisible' space, since the farmers relied on the fact that the natives were on their private property and should therefore follow the orders of the farmer. On the farm, the farmer was the law and the law was violence; hence the argument by Mrs L. Kraft (a friend of Carlson's) that there were many cases that the law could not cover in South Africa.[35]

At the same time, there were state officials like De Beer who used the law to send many Black people to the farms 'unlawfully'. That was why, in their report on pass offenders and farm labour, Van Wyk and Ngakane argued that many Black people were suspicious of the law even though they might not fully understand it.[36] Equally, they were also afraid of going to jail, so if an opportunity presented itself to avoid prison – and that 'opportunity' was the farm – they might choose it. Yet the farm took the form of a prison and the farmer was the law; and to the farmer, the language understood by the native was violence.

By shifting the focus beyond law to violence, my aim is to show that the use of violence on South African farms reflected an anxiety about the future in a country where white people are a minority. It is no wonder, then, that the liberals saw the South African agrarian problem as a problem of race. John Higginson, in the book *Collective Violence and the Agrarian Origins of South African Apartheid, 1900–1948*, argues that at face value:

> People rarely risk their lives for abstractions such as colonialism, nationalism, or white supremacy. Rather such ideals become normative standards for continuously reassessing real needs and capacities. Can I insure my family's welfare now and in the future? Am I self-sufficient? ... The most palpable expression of these questions and aspirations was rural Afrikaners' consistent demand for *boerestand*, an economic safety net out of which no rural white household could fall [emphasis in the original].[37]

The concept of a 'boerestand' is linked to what I see as a collective memory of the Afrikaners dating back to the Anglo-Boer War, when they vowed they would never again be dispossessed. Because of the trauma of the war and the resulting crisis, which saw many Afrikaners becoming landless and poor, their political struggle expressed itself through seizing the land to establish a boerestand. Hence:

> Despite deep and persisting economic divisions within the white population, they sought to create a political climate in which violence committed on behalf of a more parochial conception of private

property – what was popularly known as a *boerestand* – could be joined to the task of resurrecting white supremacy. Moreover, they wanted to ensure that their conception of private property would not only be viewed as normal but as indispensable.[38]

Higginson indicates that this collective memory/trauma created a race that was always willing to use violence to defend the land/farm. Thus, one cannot comprehend why the farm is a violent terrain without an understanding of the possibility of a return of 'colonial invasion', which may render the Afrikaner landless, or of how Black resistance is potentially dangerous since it might mean Black people want to uproot them from the land. This was an ontological anxiety always reflected in the question of Afrikaners making a home for themselves in this foreign land (remember the Voortrekkers also saw Bethal burn).

However, this anxiety was suffered not only by the Afrikaners, but by the entire white society (Afrikaners and the British in South Africa). This point is elaborated by Anthony Marx, who states that the 'issue of how to construct a racial order was central to the historical process of nation-state consolidation'.[39] He argues that in South Africa after the Anglo-Boer War, it would have been easy for the English to side with the Black people, but because of the ability of the Afrikaners to use violence against the English and the possibility of a violent revolt by the Black people, they decided to go for a white alliance. Racial 'domination had worked to diminish intrawhite conflict by bolstering the privilege and status even of poorer Afrikaners'.[40] This was not as easy as it sounds, as Higginson shows that many Afrikaners felt betrayed by the alliance which led to the formation of the Union of South Africa.

Political power was intended to secure what the Afrikaners constructed as a precarious future under foreign domination. Francis Wilson contends, 'No one who wishes to understand the history of South Africa in the century that followed the discovery of diamonds can ignore the *platteland*. For the *platteland* was the cradle of Afrikaner life and nationalism.'[41] Politically, there was the looming threat that white people in South Africa were a minority and the natives were a majority. All differences were set aside to attend to this problem. By making Black people criminals, the white society had already seen its future: in a country where a majority of Black people were turned into criminals seeking freedom from the tyranny of the white minority rule, whites' minority status was to be their downfall.

The spectre of the human potato haunts the white farmer's future

On the farm, the question was not only one of labour. It was also a question of the future of belonging to the land. With the future in mind, brutality is necessary to create conditions of docility, where Black people do not, and will not ever, speak back. In the preface to Frantz Fanon's *The Wretched of the Earth*, Jean-Paul Sartre reminds us of the important role of violence in the conquest of the world – and at the same time its failure to exist in totality/futurity:

> Violence in the colonies does not only have its aim in the keeping of these enslaved men at arm's length; it seeks to dehumanize them ... Sheer physical fatigue will stupefy them. Starved and ill, if they have any spirit left, fear will finish the job; guns are levelled at the peasant; civilians come to take over his land and force him by dint of flogging to till the land for them. If he shows fight, the soldiers fire and he's a dead man; if he gives in, he degrades himself and he is no longer a man at all; shame and fear will split up his character and make his inmost self fall to pieces ... And yet, in spite of all these efforts, their ends are nowhere achieved ... I do not say that it is impossible to change a man into an animal: I simply say that you won't get there without weakening him considerably.[42]

Violence could not kill all the workers. The spectre of the human potato reminds the farmer of the limits of violence. Patrick Duncan, in his once-banned book *South Africa's Rule of Violence*, argues 'that a special form of cruelty is produced when one group which is powerless is handed over into the power of another group, and when hostility exists between the two groups. This special form of cruelty cannot for obvious reasons be committed by Africans in South Africa against whites.'[43] Duncan's characterisation of apartheid is that of a moral degeneration in the hearts of whites who use violence to protect their interests. He covers issues of genetics, love for the other, the Group Areas Act, education, the Immorality Act and religion to show how the violence of apartheid operated to create the belief that one race was superior and the other inferior, and how under such conditions the use of violence was justified. To him, this violence was irrational since it tried to conceal the moral degeneration of white South Africans. He argued that they 'too are psychologically twisted by this inhumane system. Even when the white assailant comes out of the fight a physical victor, as he does nearly always, he comes out a spiritual cripple.'[44] In Duncan's view, the violence reflected the fact that the anxiety of white people had reached a level where it crippled them spiritually.

I have not touched on the resistance politics that might have made the white people and the state anxious about the future. For Black people were not docile; they resisted this violence, as those who wrote about resistance in South Africa have showed.[45] One explanation for the killings of farm workers could be fear of Black resistance as it was expressing itself countrywide, and the belief that the use of violence would act as a deterrent to any contestation about the future. It is a plausible argument. Much more important, however, is that while the farmers positioned themselves as owners of the land, the same land was occupied by workers and families who regarded it as their home. The same land fed them and sheltered them. They would die and be buried on the land. Therefore, the land was their eschatological future, where their spirits would rest and to which their bodies would be returned.

Chapter 5 | These eyes are looking for a home

> I believe there is no society of any kind in the Colonies, nothing that
> I would call society; so when you have made your fortune you must
> come back and assert yourself in London. — Oscar Wilde[1]

The starting point in defining the ontological category of being Black
is usually from its negative – that is to say, from what being Black
is not – to arrive at a defence of what it is. It is a difficult definition to
make. The negative ontological categories show a people wounded in
time. For a Black person, time is a shifting terrain that the condition of
dispossession helps to situate. The wound of Black people binds them
collectively and negatively into a future where they are again victims of
a past that did not see them as human. This negative ontological category makes the subject of Blackness indeterminate when the future is
mentioned.

Is there a collective state of being that binds all Black people in
South Africa under the sociological category 'a society'? I provide a
sociological reading of dispossession to answer this question, drawing
on a theoretical standpoint which positions the eye as an ethical tool for
understanding history. At the same time, I move from the framework of
the optical as ethical to look at 'society'. The history of dispossession has
been centred on white society and its fears of the future projected onto
the negative ontological category of Black. In this pursuit, I let go of the
Manicheanism already inherited from those who wrote of the 'black'

or the 'white' because I have already constructed the Manicheanism. However, in proceeding with the optical I use my eye not only as an eye belonging to the wounded collective, but as an eye concerned with the future, an eye of the Black intellectual. I have positioned dispossession as a construction of the future that maintains this negative ontological category of a Black person who has been wandering to nowhere.

My concern is not only to offer a different understanding of the question of land in South Africa; my eye is also an eye of a haunted being, who is not innocent in the reading of history, haunted by the dead (like Gogo Mshanelo, whom we met in chapter 2). Unlike Mshanelo, I cannot provide the dead with the peace and justice that they need. I am haunted not by the injustice of the past, but by the present need to understand the futurity of dispossession and the anxiety it conceals in South Africa. I turn to the living beings to understand that struggle of working and living in the violent land, haunted by the condition of ontological nowhereness.

In ontological nowhereness, we are dealing with a horrendous past that is still present. But the imagined future of this collective has not been explored – why Black people proceeded to wander into nowhere, not compromising in certain contexts, seeing all that they owned and created vanish into a vortex of dreams, dreams of a place, a home, a family, of wealth, stability and offspring. And, ultimately, they continued to ponder their future concerning land and their homelessness in death. This death is related to being a slave, a k____r.

In this chapter I approach the sociological reading of dispossession in three ways. First, there is the question of the identity ascribed to Black people, that negative ontological category of being a k____r, and what it means in terms of the difficulty of forming a social collective on the farms. Because of this negative method of identification, the Black person suffered from trauma and a desire to move away from the present.

Second, there is the matter of how, through violence, the farmers were offering a particular form of education to the farmworkers and their children. This education, which was grounded in violence, merely concealed the anxiety of the farmers, who wanted to shape a future in which Black people on the farms remained docile.

Third, I want to relate this to the 'state', that entity which is an expression and protection of the identity of the members of society. My argument is that there was no Black society. Even the state did not recognise Black people as belonging to a society, leaving many farmworkers desiring a state to protect their interests. This desire for a state is a desire for a future in which Black people can define themselves. The state is always reflective of this nationalistic desire; the apartheid state aimed to assuage the anxieties of the white society by ensuring that it distinguished white people from the 'inferior' Black people. Apartheid was about cementing a home for white people in South Africa.

The search for a home is a search for a place of rest, a place of a spiritual collective identity, a place that will not only shelter the family but will also protect the collective – a place for the future in 'a land of tyrants, and a den of slaves, where wretches seek dishonourable graves'.[2]

'You are k____rs, you are monkeys ...'

Julien Benda argues that in the history of humanity the emergence of a society is driven by two goals: the pursuit of material interests and the collective desire of the members of that society to distinguish themselves.[3] These are the positive ontological interests that come to shape the collective and its desire to control its destiny or future. Think, for example, of the Marxian explanation of class struggle, the proletariat against the bourgeoisie, each seeking to protect their material interests and bring forth a particular state of existence, a society fashioned on those interests. At the same time, the collective's ability to distinguish itself is not only linked to material interests, but also speaks to a desire to shape the future.

In using this framework in relation to the question of dispossession, we learn that indeed there is a material interest that binds Black people in South Africa: dispossession. What we fail to see is Black people's collective interest in distinguishing themselves in the world. Even this interest of dispossession did not bind all Black people. In the history of dispossession in South Africa, there was a certain stratum of Black people who formed a movement in 1912 to represent the interests of educated Black people as subjects of the British Empire so that they could purchase land. As No Sizwe (Neville Alexander) observed:

> Land was, until approximately 1948, the crucial factor around which a white-black conflict could arise. However, the monopoly of power enjoyed by whites ruled out any possibility of the inarticulate, disorganised and disunited blacks constituting any serious threat to the status quo.[4]

Even Black Consciousness fails to solve the negative ontological problem, since it defines being Black as a mental state of resistance and a desire to transcend the negative ontological categories of being Black. Thus, to the world, many who wear the pigmentation of Black but who have not come to the consciousness of resistance may be seen merely as non-white. Resistance does not mean a shared positive category, but a reaction and a method of refutation. The ideas that lionise the state of being Black may be used in an attempt to foster a particular intellectual and political movement, one which not all Black people become part of. That is, trying to build political consciousness to transcend the negative ontological category that sees Black people as lacking 'ontological resistance'[5] does not mean that there is a distinguished collective.

For Black people who are dispossessed of their land, what does it mean to be Black in the condition of nowhereness and how do they use their situation to distinguish themselves? Do they share the same desire to distinguish themselves as a collective? How do they distinguish themselves? Not seeing a shared collective desire that links their material interests and the aspiration to distinguish themselves as a collective does not mean that this is impossible in the future. Because of dispossession, Black people can be wounded without accountability because this wound is not a wound to society – a Black society does not exist – but a wound to an unidentified being. That is why the use of violence on the farms was always justified, and the burying of the dead as if they were dogs was not regarded as peculiar by the farmers.

I draw on the transcripts of interviews conducted by Dr Tshepo Moloi in 2007–2008 to understand the history of Bethal and the violence that took place on the farms. All the interviews contain variations of this sentiment: that as 'k____rs' (a negative ontological category), farmworkers could be set to work at little or no pay, violated, and children would see their parents whipped in front of them by the farmer. The words in the subheading above – 'You are k____rs, you are monkeys' – are those of Elizabeth Mkhwanazi, who was born and raised on a farm in Bethal. All interviewees are haunted by these words – that a k____r is a slave to the land, working from sunrise to sunset, with no place to call home, always at the mercy of the farm owner. Sometimes the workers could bathe only on weekends in a man-made dam. This was life on the farm:

> When you were sick, you could not stay at home and treat your ailment or go to the doctor. You would just go to work like that. When it was time for a break, you would be feeling so much pain, you couldn't even eat because of the pain. Rather you used that time to nurse your pains and await the whistle to blow. And then you resumed working again. Then came a time when I asked myself why I was working so hard? Why I can't just die so that this pain can go away? I thought about something, but I did not succeed doing it. I tried to hang myself. I took a rope and tied it at the back of the house, then I put it around my neck and stood on top of something. As I was about to climb my friend came out and asked me what I was doing. I just became aggressive and told her to leave me alone.[6]

Elizabeth Mkhwanazi, in this state of ontological nowhereness, unable to escape the life on the farm and not knowing any place to find refuge, tried to commit suicide. Her depression was linked to what she saw on the farm: workers killed and their bodies buried like dogs, violent abuse, being hit in the face with potatoes if one tried to rest. Death for her meant that she would be freed from this individual pain that she seemed to share with many on the farm, but about which they could not speak together. This pain is associated with the negative ontological category of a k____r. As a k____r, a slave to the land, she had no other way of imagining herself beyond being subjected to the violence on the farm and the possibility of dying at any moment. This was her future, where violence reminded all workers that they would die like dogs. She longed to escape, but she knew no other home. In death, she hoped that the pain would finally go away.

Ironically, it was the subject of death that exposed the violence on the farms, for the dead came back as potatoes, no longer haunting only those on the farms, but haunting the entire South African landscape.

The accounts by Mkhwanazi and the others interviewed offer a heuristic model of the trauma. The violence on the farm haunted all the interviewees. Death was reserved not just for the prison labourers or the 'ama joints' (contract or immigrant workers). Death was ubiquitous for all who worked the land. However, through the eyes of Mkhwanazi we see a desire for a self to distinguish itself, through suicide, to find peace and escape the oppressive conditions. This act was an individual response to the collective trauma. Mkhwanazi survived a suicide attempt, but she was still confronted by the death of other farmworkers:

> After that it was difficult to look at them [farm labourers]. When I looked at them my eyes would be filled with tears. It invoked misery in me when I thought that my people were being killed and they were not even buried properly. They were just taking their corpses in mass [sic] and putting them inside the graves without coffins. And we were also suffering. There was no light at the end of the tunnel and *we seemed to be stuck in one place* [emphasis added].[7]

This was an organised form of life on the farm. It entailed controlling the life cycle of the Black people, since 'farmers not only expect Natives to render them free labour, but they actually wish the Natives to breed slaves for them'.[8] This control of life and death was part and parcel of the agricultural system of labour tenancy, which was a system of familial subjugation, ensuring that the children paid for their parents' sins – of being landless and being born Black.

In the correspondence of V.S. Welsford to the Native Commissioner/ Office of the Magistrate (Carolina), a letter dated 8 December 1953 addresses the SAIRR.[9] Welsford and his wife had employed a 'boy' by the name of Hamilton Ncongwane to do general work as a caretaker at their homestead and their Mensana Book Publishers warehouse. Mr Ncongwane, the father of Hamilton, was a labour tenant in Bethal, on a farm owned by Hendrick de Clercq. De Clercq needed someone to herd his cattle, and he sent Mr Ncongwane to fetch his son to fill this gap. In his letters, Mr Welsford indicated that he would send someone else to carry out the task that Hamilton was supposed to perform, but Mr Ncongwane insisted that Hamilton must come or else the family would face eviction. Frustrated, Mr Welsford wrote to the SAIRR to complain that 'de Clercq regarded the natives on his farm as an asset to be disposed of at his pleasure! Slavery?' Welsford hit the nail on the head. Such control of human life is slavery. His benevolent attempt to rescue Hamilton failed, however, and the magistrate ordered the boy back to Bethal. This was because the 'Roman Dutch Law and Native Customary Law favour the retention of the system' and allowed for control of parents over their minor sons.[10] No one could pay Ncongwane's debt to De Clercq except his blood: Hamilton. This kind of treatment even extended to the squatters' sons. The chain of letters indicates that farmers in Andover and Leamington served eviction orders on those who refused to send their sons to work for the farmer, even if they were paying rent and their boys were attending school.

These examples underscore that on the farm there was no self-definition, which is an important aspect of what makes a society. This ability to self-define is also that which shapes the desire of the collective to distinguish itself. On the farm, children were tied to their parents, and their parents were tied to the farmer. At the same time, this arrangement has been termed the paternalism of South African farming.[11] This paternalism is about an identity that is also tied to the home, the primary space of socialisation.

Black people had no independent home on the farm because they were 'children of the white farmer'. Social relations perpetuated the negation of the farm labourers for the future of the white farmer. The Black majority on this farm did not constitute a society. For that, they needed those positive ontological categories of having clearly identified material interests and a desire to distinguish themselves. However, this state of being is not a permanent state, since it always relates to the future, which is not fixed. Because the desire to establish a collective is always present, it does not mean that violence stops it eternally, as I argued in chapter 4. That is why today the question of land approaches us as a present-future, in the sense that it represents a nascent collective desire to define a self in relation to the land, and to build a collective identity around the state of being dispossessed. This present-future is linked to the past. The past is linked to the negative ontological category related to being landless, and the future is linked to the issue of the return of land to its rightful owners to create a positive distinguishable collective identity.

Educating through violence

The ability to self-define is linked to socialisation, hence the question of land being linked to the making of a home. To make a home also means a need for institutions to sustain it – which is why education as a secondary tool of socialisation is necessary. Education on the farm was enforced through violence to inculcate a negative image of self, and the bond between parents and children existed merely to serve the farmer. Children in these conditions always desired a better future. Even for Mkhwanazi, this better future was to be free from bondage – albeit, ironically, through death, and in her case through suicide. The very same death that had traumatised her on the farm was what she desired to carry her out of bondage on the farm.

Violence was inflicted on the entire Black family structure and Black children were present as witnesses to their parents' denigration. There is no positive self-image for a growing child whose parent is rendered useless in front of their eyes, made fragile, incapable of protecting the future of their family. Even worse, such a parent cannot be expected to shape their family and infuse good family values. As Mr Nsibande put it, '[O]ur fathers were oppressed until they died on these farms.'[12] This was a form of primary socialisation seeking to mould a particular identity, a docile being, one who would never contest a future since they would not have a positive reference of self. The potential power of a good education is to help the individual locate their self-identity in the chain of humanity deserving to be treated with dignity and respect. All the interviewees attested that they had never received proper schooling on the farms. Their parents' attempts at ensuring that their children received a good education were met with beatings. Mkhwanazi's encounter with the farmer when he found out that her father was secretly sending her to school is telling:

[W]hen I started school, eh, it was clear on the farm that kids were not supposed to go to school. They must work together with the men. My father tried by all means that my younger sister and I should continue schooling. My sister and I are a few years apart. He sneaked us out through the back so that we could go to school. The school was at eNkundleni. The people on the farm were speaking about this until it reached the farmer's attention that Paulos' kids were attending school. Then one Sunday the farm owner and his son arrived. They were driving in a car. They stopped the car and called my father outside and said: 'Yes, Paulos, I heard that your kids are going to school.' He said: 'No, boss. My kids are not going to school.' He [the farmer] said: 'I have been informed!' They then got off the car – they even brought dogs. They beat my father up and eventually he conceded and said that: 'Yes, boss, I was just doing it unlawfully.' He [the farmer] then told my father that he wanted us at work. My father told him that he would bring us with him.[13]

Education also involved the intervention of the state, or the promotion of policy to ensure that Black people attained an education on the farm. For example, the SAAU, one of the institutions considered by the SAIRR to be 'progressive', launched its 'Native Policy for Agriculture', in which one can see the discourse of treating the native as a human being.[14] The recommendations and questions posed by the SAAU policy are like those raised by the first director of the SAIRR, John David Rheinallt Jones.[15] The policy discussed education and training, the availability of health facilities on the farm for the native, better housing and nutrition, better remuneration and the improvement of working conditions. 'The Union realises that the native male has a definite innate or cultivated attitude towards manual labour and feels that farmers should organise their labour in such a manner that the worker has certain free hours during the week for his own affairs or recreation.'[16] The policy was ordered around cultivating the abilities of the native males and ensuring that they remained on the farm. The SAAU argued that these questions of modernising agriculture needed to be understood in tandem with South Africa's history of paternalism within a system of guardianship:

[T]he relationship between employer and employee particularly in the case of the permanent labourer and his family on the farm, will continue to be the traditional one of guardian and protégé … It is therefore in the light of this relationship, which is the natural outcome of geographical factors and a development of human relations extending over many years, that the Union has consistently formulated its policy in regard to Native labour.[17]

The policy stated that farmers should build schools on their premises for the education of the native children (the same recommendation made by the SAIRR). It also promoted the erection of other institutions of modernity, including clinics and prisons. The policy was against the petty offenders' scheme, arguing that it turned farmers into jailers, as they erected prisons on the farms to benefit from the overcrowding in the country's prisons. Farmers had no interest in the positive outcomes of these proposed institutions of modernity; they wished only to harness prison labour to deal with the twentieth-century problem of labour shortages. Jails took precedence over schools because they lent themselves more easily to rationalising violence; they entailed the use of overt violence whereas educational institutions leaned towards covert violence. Jails concentrated on punishment, whereas schools focused on empowering labourers with the skills required on the farm. Ultimately, SAAU argued that

> Christianity, humanity and justice should always be the mainspring of the farmer's dealings with his labourer. In this respect, every citizen, including the farmer, can make a great contribution to the creation of a happier community and to better racial relations in this multi-racial country of ours.[18]

This scenario could not have been further from the reality of life on the farms.

In the time of apartheid Black people had no political-institutional voice/representation, and separate development was seen as a solution to the problem of proximity between the races in South Africa. The SAIRR was formed in 1929 in order to

> work for peaceful and practical co-operation between the various sections and races of the South African population. One of its goals was ... to research realities of the time[,] study the facts of current situations in order, if possible, to ensure the elimination of causes of inter-group friction.[19]

When the question of farm labour emerges within the historical archive, it is always grounded in this preoccupation with the welfare of the country. The issue of farm labour was seen as one that might affect race relations in future, and reports produced by the SAIRR – such as 'Labour in the Farm Economy' by Margaret Robert[20] and 'Farm Labour in the Transvaal' by Edith Rheinallt Jones[21] – were directed to those who were interested in understanding the labour question or the shortage of labour in South Africa. These reports focused on how workers were coping even as they were made to stay on the farm so that white farmers would benefit from their labour. The reports are part of a discursive making of the Black farmworker, a metaphysics of representation, through the eyes of the benevolent white liberal, addressing white society and the state.

The 'progressive language' expressed the idea of educating both the parent and the child to reorient their views regarding labour and industriousness. The language of education was a form of violence that no longer spoke of punishment but emphasised the capital good of education for the African child, enhancing the contribution of Black children to the farm or the economy in general. Such discourse proposed a continuity of violence that was not overt, and required a different understanding of work to be accepted by 'lazy natives'. In fact, farmers had no genuine interest in the wellbeing and education of their workers. One farmer told a teacher to release children during school hours because he wanted them 'now before they are exhausted. If you give them to me after school, I will first have to feed them.'[22]

This discursive making of the Black farmworker works in two ways: through the present and through the future. First, the question of the present was how to bind Black workers to the farm to keep them from going to the city. We see here an argument about fostering a different relationship that Black people are supposed to have with the land. Second, regarding the question of the future, Black children would remain harnessed to the farms as new generations of labourers. Ultimately, paternalism on South African farms conceals the ontological problem: Black people could not be considered responsible beings – responsible for themselves, their families and their 'society'. The language of paternalism affirms the argument of the non-existent Black society that is forced to be under the guardianship of the fictitious violent white father. As Mkhwanazi puts it:

> [C]an you talk to the king? We didn't say anything. We didn't even look at him. We could hear in our ears that he was talking, but we would never answer him or even look at him. We would be inviting death.[23]

Paternalism contributes to moulding the narrative of the ontologically lacking figure of a Black person. In this narrative construction, such a figure cannot be trusted with matters of the land since the land relates to the future. Indeed, the language of paternalism conceals the anxious white father who uses violence not only to thwart resistance but to conceal the illegitimate status of fatherhood that rests on the idea of absolute rights to the land.

A contested state

The apartheid state protected white fatherhood and granted it legitimacy to reduce its anxiety. The state not only possessed a monopoly on violence, being the arbiter of law and order; it also concealed the tyranny of white society in South Africa. This was to ensure that there was no emergence of a Black society to contest the future of this already precarious state of existence of a minority imposing itself over a majority. Yet the majority was struggling, struggling to find its face under the tyrannical conditions, to find ways of expressing its being. On the farms, as Mr Mahlangu indicates, they knew they had no state to protect them:

> [B]ecause the government belonged to the whites. You could not report them. They would tell you that you were mad, go back to work. Even when the white man provoked you and you beat him

up, you could get into trouble. You had no right to beat a white man. Who could defend you?[24]

The violence, the law and the state collaborated to protect the identity of white society.

However, this social engineering did not mean that the South African state was not contested by Black resistance. Consider the potato boycott of June–September 1959.[25] This boycott was a loud shout from a people assumed to be mute, with leaders like Gert Sibande said to be always emphasising 'Mayibuye iAfrica' (Africa come back). 'Our country must come back.'[26] Almost three decades before the boycott, Sibande had begun to organise farmworkers. In the 1930s, he formed the Farmworkers' Association to protect labour tenants against abusive farmers. He was also politically aligned with the ANC, which took the decision to launch a national mass campaign in which South Africans would be urged not to eat potatoes. The slogan 'Mayibuye iAfrica' was part of the Africanist turn[27] in the liberation struggle during the 1950s:

> [Mayibuye iAfrica] became a common call, or shout, during 1959. The sense of identification with the continent that it expressed was dramatized on Africa Day, April 15, the first anniversary of the first Accra Conference of Independent African States. Celebrations were organized during the week of April 12–19. In Johannesburg on April 15 a float symbolizing Africa moved through the central part of the city and African areas, and 'Freedom' placards were displayed on the City Hall steps.[28]

The catalyst for the potato boycott was the death of Cornelius Mokgoko, who was 24 years of age when he died on the Legdaar farm belonging to R. Meiring, who asked Johannes Shumbo to help bury him.[29] Those who have covered the potato boycott argue that it should be located within the formation of the African political consciousness that was grounded in the basic tactics of the Congress Alliance.[30] The argument is that after the adoption of the Freedom Charter in 1955, there was a need to

> organize the Blacks around local issues which affected their daily lives, and then explain the interlinking of those issues with the basic problems confronting Blacks … to make people aware [of] their local grievances … The campaign led to improved conditions for the workers.[31]

Billy Nair, a member of the Congress Alliance, does not deviate from the view of locating the boycott within the formation of the political consciousness of the oppressed when he states that the boycott, which also involved the South African Congress of Trade Unions, resulted in '60 000 people attend[ing] the … rally at Currie's Fountain in Durban'.[32] As the boycott got under way, the *Star* newspaper ran an article reporting that a number of farmers were bringing truckloads of workers back to the labourer bureaus.[33] On 17 June 1959, the *Rand Daily Mail* carried an account of how the boycott was affecting potato sales.[34]

Thus, the boycott happened against the backdrop of several protests that were led by Black people trying to fight the oppressive nature of the apartheid state. This resistance was against restricted mobility at home, similar to the 1955 resistance in Sophiatown[35] and the 1956 women's march against the pass laws. There were also the 'anti-poverty' strikes such as the 1957 bus boycott in Alexandra and the pound-a-day campaign in 1957.[36] In June 1959, an anti-pass riot broke out in Cato Manor in Durban and other areas of Natal in protest against forced removals; it led to the death of nine policemen.[37] On 21 March 1960, protests led by the Pan Africanist Congress (PAC) resulted in the Sharpeville Massacre. The PAC had broken away from the ANC, arguing for the self-assertion and self-reliance of Black people.

It is not the case that such moments of resistance never reached the farms. These protests and boycotts not only shook the state but also made the entire white society concerned about the danger of Black people (swart gevaar). Thus, such moments can be read as a desire by Black people to forge a collective identity based on shared material interests. This aspiration, a desire for a future Black society, always threatened white society as a whole.

The national resistance involving Black people meant that the future was contested, a prospect that agitated all of white society. Indeed, the 1950s represented a period of intense global challenge against white-supremacist capitalist European domination in Africa and the African diaspora.[38] The period is also characterised as the heyday of apartheid, when racial laws that sought to partition South Africans by race were passed or tightened. Among others, the following laws were passed: the Prohibition of Mixed Marriages Act of 1949, outlawing marriage between whites and 'non-whites'; the Immorality Act of 1950, which prohibited sexual relations between whites and Black people; the Population Registration Act in 1950, which classified people in South Africa according to four races – white, coloured, Bantu (Black African) and other. There was also an intervention to separate residential areas by race under the Group Areas Act of 1950. Such legislation represents a significant expression of the global anxiety of whiteness in the face of resistance and change.

For reforms were happening on the global stage. In December 1948, the United Nations adopted the Universal Declaration of Human Rights.[39] Almost a decade later, a period of decolonisation was sparked in Africa when Ghana gained its independence in 1957. In the USA, Black people intensified their anti-colonial struggle through the civil rights movement. This is what Ralph Ellison calls 'an identity of passions' reflecting the crossing of 'national and cultural boundaries' of resistance by Black people.[40] Such resistance was coupled with what were known as the 'peasant wars' of the twentieth century in countries such as Russia, Mexico, China, Algeria, Kenya, Cuba and Vietnam.[41] Such struggles spoke to the core of the land struggle by the rural oppressed, a struggle to eat from the land and establish a home for the dispossessed.

The struggle of the Black peasants in South Africa was summarised by Govan Mbeki:

> Between 1946 and 1962 risings have been provoked in Witzies-hoek, on the border of Basutoland; in Marico, just south of Bechuanaland; in Sekhukhuneland, in the north-west Transvaal; in Zululand, on the South Coast; and throughout the Transkei, especially in Pondoland. They have been suppressed with brutal force.[42]

This period led to heightened use of violence by the South African state. At the ideological level, the state passed the Suppression of Communism Act of 1950, banning the Communist Party of South Africa; later, in the 1960s, it banned all Black political parties. The 1960s saw a hiatus in the resistance politics of South Africa: for a decade, there was silence. Resistance re-emerged when Black dockworkers went on strike in Durban in 1969, later in the factories in Durban in 1973, and later still, beginning on 16 June 1976, when schoolchildren, galvanised by the Black Consciousness movement, protested against the Bantu Education Act of 1953. Mkhwanazi recalls:

> In 1976 things were bad. It was the time when the kids in Soweto were being killed during the Black Power. Things became tough for us. We were warned against talking about what was happening to us. There was one woman who told us what was happening and she wanted us to talk about what was happening. The news got to the white farmers and she was taken away to be locked up in town. She came back after some time and she was informed that she couldn't say anything. We were all told to keep quiet.[43]

These eyes are looking for a home

Beyond the national and global resistance that was already shaking the South African landscape, there was one thing that always bothered the farmers: the Black farmworkers recognised the farm as their home. As Mahlangu indicates:

> Being on the farm was like you were at home. As long as you have built your home on the white man's farm you continued work-ing there. There was no relocating those days. You would start by building a house, get married, and have a family. The whole family would work for the white man. People remained on the farm and brought up their children who also worked on the farm, and the homestead will grow. You would end up having a big family and a big homestead. That is what they began to fight for, claiming that this was my place of birth, my place of origin.[44]

The squatters' children whose parents paid rent to the farmer, the daughters of the labour tenants who were denied schooling, the ama joints and the prison labourers who were kept on the farm for longer than they had anticipated – all began to see the farm as their home. As wretched as their living and working conditions were, they refused to turn their eyes elsewhere. This heightened the fear of the white farmers that the resistance politics outside their gates was bound to enter their farms if they did not use force to control their workers. For many Black people, as Mahlangu notes, the farm, no matter how violent, was their place of birth. In the future, they would contest this place of birth, call-ing it their home, their past, their link with the ancestors buried on the land, and the rightful home of their offspring.

Chapter 6 | Bethal today

In moving to the present, it becomes clear that the ontological nowhere-ness characterised as the search for somewhere to live and die represents the ongoing resistance against being landless. As we move to the present, we arrive at the condition of a place that exists somewhere, a place called home, a place where the dead rest and a place where the living will also rest when they are dead. This is the Bethal of today, a Bethal of the present, where contestation reflects an ongoing historical cycle, where the present always reflects our past. Our present is a historical present – a past present with us, whose presence represents the unresolved history of our present spiritual moment. To visit Bethal today, in the present, is to revisit the past. The violence of dispossession entails an eschatological gaze, which means that the spirit of the past remains in this land.

I have been arguing that we do not need to see the land only through an economic lens. To see it as such is a form of debasement that renders us part of the ontology of violence of ownership which conceals anxiety about the future. To visit Bethal today is to arrive at the future. That is why when Jürgen Schadeberg (the renowned photographer who was a friend and colleague of Henry Nxumalo at the time of the *Drum* exposé) visited Bethal in April 2005 with Styles Ledwaba, they were to write that '53 years after Nxumalo's exposé ... although the whips and the forced labour are gone, farmworkers in the area face a struggle of a different kind'.[1] Schadeberg had been familiar with Bethal since 1952, when, with

Nxumalo, he had posed as a German tourist and had managed to take some pictures of the compounds. Schadeberg also helped Nxumalo escape from the farm that was part of the subsequent *Drum* story, where he had taken pictures of farmworkers carrying sacks of potatoes in the field. Another picture was of a 'boss-boy' with a whip riding a horse in a maize field (see figure 3.2).[2]

In going to Bethal today, I am going to the places where the violence took place, to understand the spiritual meaning of this past in the present and the future (see figure 6.1 showing the farms visited). I am not alone. Xender Ehlers is my interlocutor, taking me to the farms. He was born in Bethal, but he came to see the place differently when he began to read and hear the stories of the area (this evolution is a story he will tell one day). We went to Legdaar farm, where the 24-year-old Cornelius Mokgoko was subjected to violence for days, where he was told that in Bethal, if an animal does not work they throw it out. Then we went to Schurvekop, the farm Ledwaba and Schadeberg had visited in 2005 and where they found that labour tenants were being pushed off the land. There they had encountered Vusi, who insisted that the tenants would not be moved because 'this is our land. I can't tell what's going to happen if someone tries to move me. But I can tell you, something will happen that day. Something will happen.'[3] From Vusi's statements, we thought it would be important to visit the farm, and I indicated to Xender that it spoke to the issue that my book was attending to: the future. What does this future look like if we visit Bethal 16 years after the visit by Schadeberg and Ledwaba, 69 years after Nxumalo's visit and 74 years after the Reverend Michael Scott's visit? On my visit to Schurvekop, I realised that farming is no longer the main activity as now there is a coal mine. At Schurvekop, I met Moses Magwaza (not his real name), who told me that he was seeing the future of this land – where there is no farm work and the children leave their parents and their dead behind. I then went to Kalabasfontein, where Reverend Scott recounted the trial in the magistrate's court in which a certain foreman, Balthasar Johannes Brenkman of Kalabasfontein, was found guilty of assault with intent

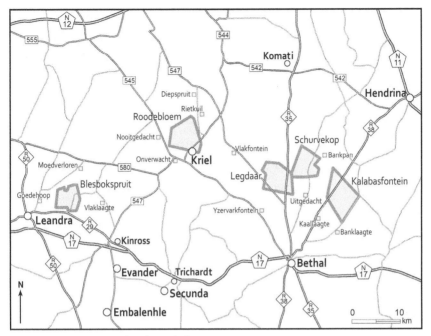

Figure 6.1: Farms visited in the Bethal area

to inflict grievous bodily harm.[4] There are two farms where we suspect that Henry Nxumalo might have worked for his exposé for *Drum*,
Blesbokspruit and Roodebloem. The farm mentioned by Schadeberg
in his memoir *The Way I See it*, 'Sonneblom Plaas–Van der Merwe–
Privaat',[5] could not be found in the title deeds archive. The best way was
to continue to follow how Schadeberg saw the land and we did this by
visiting a farm he went to, Blesbokspruit, with the hope that this might
be 'Sonneblom'. In Blesbokspruit, Ledwaba and Schadeberg had met a
labour tenant, Sarah, who had been on the land for 18 years and was
being pushed out by the farmer. It was her son who commented: 'This
is my only home. I grew up here and I'm going nowhere.' For this reason, the farm had become an interesting space – it spoke to the core
theme of this book: home and the making of a home. We also went to
Roodebloem farm (there is a similarity with the name 'Sonneblom'), but
we found no clues that could help us determine whether this was the
farm where Nxumalo had worked. On Blesbokspruit we did discover

a compound, however, and Mr Mahlangu, who was born on the farm, indicated that the building had been used to house prison labourers. It is plausible, therefore, that this is the farm on which the *Drum* exposé was based.

'Bethal Today' was the headline to an article written by Nxumalo in 1952. In writing this chapter, I build on the tradition of 'today' by adding aspects of the present (today). However, in going to Bethal today, I am arguing that even today we are looking into a historical present, a past that always remains present. For Nxumalo and for Scott, the past-present nexus was that the violence in Bethal could be dated as far back as the 1920s, when a farmer was found guilty of binding a worker by the feet to a tree and thrashing him to death. Looking at the farming fields of Bethal, Scott thought that slavery was more humane than what was happening in Bethal, while Ruth First was to add that Bethal was responsible for the 'jumble sale' of human beings.[6]

In looking at Bethal, I have drawn from the philosophy of Emmanuel Levinas the idea that the eye is an ethical organ that sees the face of the Other and responds to a demand not to kill. This demand is eschatological, for the face of the Other carries with it the spirit of the Other. I have argued that this means that we need to write the question of the land Otherwise, to see not only the face of the Other and its demand, but also the spirit of the land. When the workers were looking at the land, they were using an eschatological gaze. I go beyond this theory of alterity, which in itself is anthropocentric, for the face of the Other is positioned as a spiritual entity that is visible. In the end, my eye is also guilty; it is the eye of a scholar, who is also concerned with the importance of theorising. I hope to leave behind a theory by which we can look at the land beyond the alterity. I have argued that we can also look at the land with an eschatological gaze. I present this as a question of making a home to live in and die in. For one looking in from outside, this eschatology might mean that the process of meaning-making concerning the land is still seen within the anthropocentric utility – that is to say, the land remains useful spiritually since it is shaped by those who have a relationship with it.

The position of the eschatological gaze is that land itself is a spirit, and those working and living on the land are in conversation with that spirit. That is why the land is our eschatological future; its past refers us back to our relationship with it, with ourselves and with others. Its future still refers us back to our anxieties in the past and the present. This spirit makes itself visible to the archaeologists who, in seeking to understand humanity by looking at different points in civilisations, return to the land, go to the graves, the caves, the rocks and the trees to see how humanity related to the land (informed by chronology and genealogy).

The past remains present

I first went to Bethal in 2020, starting from the township of eMzinoni, to which some of the labour tenants who were born on the farms in northern Bethal relocated. This was the township where researcher Dr Tshepo Moloi conducted interviews with some of these labour tenants (cited in chapter 5) during 2007 and 2008. When I went to Bethal, it was difficult to trace anyone who had been alive during the farm-killings scandal. I encountered a generation who were either born in the township of eMzinoni or began working on the northern side of Bethal from the late 1970s to the 1980s. However, the labour tenants on farms today were quick to remind me that their parents had been born on the farms and had started working there in the 1920s. This confirmed for me how they saw their lives. As Mr Mathebe said, 'Farm life is all that I know.'[7]

The history of farm killings is present in their minds, but they have never worked with any prison labourers because the system was no longer in operation when they started working. Only one interlocutor, Mr Soko from eMzinoni, indicated that in the 1970s he served his sentence on a Bethal farm owned by Sydney Steyn, who was known as 'Mavuka Emini' (the one who wakes up in the afternoon). The system was not the same as it had been earlier, in the 1940s and 1950s, because there were fewer ama joints from Malawi (Nyasaland) or Transkei, but nevertheless the stories still haunt workers today. Mr Soko recounts this haunting of the past in the present:

> [O]nce when we were working the land, a tractor revealed a human skull and one of the foremen called the other. These were the guys who had worked on the farm in the 1950s or 1960s. They were old and very proud men. The one foreman says, 'Hmmm, I wonder whose skull is this.' The other one started thinking long and hard and says, 'Ahhhh, it is that Nyasa we had killed here,' and they laughed.[8]

In our conversation, Mr Soko insisted that this was what he experienced. He said he witnessed it with his own eyes and ears.

It is not the individual memory that I appeal to when looking at Bethal – because memory itself contains many sources (many minds), so it is difficult to find a consistent telling of a story – but I draw on many eyes. In *The River of Consciousness*, Oliver Sacks says this about memory:

> We, as human beings, are landed with memories which have fallibilities, frailties, and imperfections – but also great flexibility and creativity. Confusion over sources or indifference to them can be a paradoxical strength: if we could tag the sources of all our knowledge, we would be overwhelmed with often irrelevant information ... Memory arises not only from experience but from the intercourse of many minds.[9]

I see an eschatological opening in the stories told about the human potato. In considering all the farms in northern Bethal, where the labour tenants speak of encountering many unmarked graves, I cannot help but wonder whose ancestors those are. These are living dead beings, who had a past, who belonged to a people that loved them, but sadly today they lie in unmarked graves, unknown and unclaimed. When I interviewed Mr Sithole in 2021, he told me about the dead and his interpretation:

[T]he workers have ended up working during the day because the spirit of the dead continues to haunt the land and because of this haunting the spirits make people lost and wander on the farm and not do any work.[10]

Most workers on the farms believe that the lost ancestors perform chicanery, although they do not harm the living: 'They just get you lost and have you moving without any direction.'[11] Once dead, the deceased worker does not simply vanish from the face of the earth but remains as a spirit on the farm.

My interest in Bethal today is to show that this eschatological 'haunting' still speaks in this present time, and to propose another way to look at it: through a spiritual eye. I touch on the subject of law – the post-apartheid Extension of Security of Tenure Act 62 of 1997 – and show that it continues to promote the farmer as the law on the farm. When I asked the workers who resided on the farms if they had title deeds, they did not know. Their fear was that once the farm got sold it would be easy to lose their homes, and once again the search to nowhere would begin. As Mr Mazibuko said to me, 'Uzoyaphi?' (Where will you go?) The paradox of South African agriculture relates to a sense of spiritual connection, to be able to eat from the land, to be connected to the land by being buried in it and returned to one's ancestors. Yet, because of the violence and exploitation that comes with the historical fact of private property, the workers also resent being treated as 'k____rs' or slaves. Although farm labourers were without any legalised land ownership on the farms, they still regard the farm as their home.

'Uzoyaphi?' (Where will you go?)

Mr Mazibuko relayed how it was for him on the farm Legdaar amidst all the unmarked graves in the fields. I asked him how it felt to work in an area with such a dark history but which is also his place of employment and, for the most part, one that he identified with as home. He said:

> There is nothing to feel. We are working. Where will you go? There
> is nowhere to go. Where will you go? You work here and you stay
> here and you need a place to stay, a home. There is nowhere to go;
> where can you go? Even if you go to another farm, it is still the
> same ... this means you are looking for a place to live. Where will
> you find life if you do not have [a] place to stay? ... Where will you
> go? Remember in the past it was not just easy to go and stay in
> the township – you needed permission. At least now they can find
> stands in the township, but during apartheid it also meant that if
> you do not want to work on this farm, you go to another farm. But
> they are all the same.[12]

If the concept of ontological nowhereness has not yet been understood, Mr Mazibuko's account is worth consulting as it gives this concept clarity and concision, especially when he says: 'Where will you go? There is nowhere to go.' Mr Mazibuko went on to indicate that this did not mean they were happy with the living and working conditions (in the past and the present). Confronted with this condition of ontological nowhereness, they tried to make a home in this land. Remember the guilt of Mrs Hoedemaker (described in chapter 2), who asked about the state of happiness of the Bantu? It was her view that it seemed they had lost their 'natural happiness in the last years ... More in the towns than on the farms, I think but even here: is there not a bitterness in the young people's hearts, when they see, how the old ones get old?'[13] This metaphysical guilt was ameliorated by Van Wyk's response. Using similar paternalistic language, the liberal director of the SAIRR reminded Mrs Hoedemaker that Black people in the countryside were backward, reflecting a white societal chorus: 'Don't feel sorry for them ... They're happier than you and I.'[14] Those who were no longer happy were suspected of harbouring vengeful thoughts, which was what Mrs Hoedemaker was trying to get at.

The source of the unhappiness of the Black person, which is linked to ontological nowhereness, is a cause of agitation in white society. Being faced with this ontological nowhereness does not mean farmworkers have given up, for to be unhappy is to confront oneself and draw courage to think differently of the future. On the farms, the parents speak of how their children leave them to find work or study in the cities. Mr Mathebe poignantly expresses this condition:

> They [children] say they are not happy here on the farm and that the home we have created is under threat because we are always bothered by these white farm owners who are always seeking to move us from the land. They say it is better to go to the city and work and get a house in the township. What will they do in the city if they are not educated or employed? Even when they are educated, what will they do? They do not have houses; they must pay rent, and do not even have [own] a home yet. When they leave the farms, they say they are running away from oppression. Those of us in the farms eat from the land, but when you are in the city, if you do not have money, you go hungry. They will not even have places to be buried in. I will not move from the farm because this is where my parents left me when they died and this is where I will die.[15]

Mr Mathebe's homestead is one of the few houses still left on Blesbokspruit farm. His closest neighbour, Mr Mahlangu, lives two kilometres away. In our conversation with Mr Mathebe, he told us how tough it was to live on this land and that was why all the children were also unhappy. However, he would keep on fighting to be there because 'this is where my parents left me'. The Blesbokspruit farm is leased out to different farmers, and to Mr Mathebe the actions of these farmers seem to 'want to destroy life and the future'.[16] He told us that the entire field next to his house used to be covered with trees, but the farmer who had leased the land began cutting down all the trees and dumping them where cattle drank water. This type of behaviour had forced many labour tenants to leave the farm for stands in the township, which Mr Mathebe viewed as causing more suffering since they would no longer eat from the land and would have to pay for everything. He asserted that cutting down all the trees was destroying life and the future – and that the farmer was also planning to destroy his stock because by throwing the felled trees in the drinking well, the cattle would not have water to drink and could die of thirst. Mr Mathebe continued:

> How can you cut all the trees? The tree is life, the spirit of the land. I went to the town and got some lawyers who were able to assist, and they forced the farmer to remove the cut trees from the drinking well. We won and I even got an extra JoJo water tank. This made me untouchable. Sometimes you wish to tell all those who have left the farm that what the farmers are doing is unjust. Sometimes you do not want to be seen as a rabble-rouser. I know that by doing all these tricks they are making sure that there is no one here tomorrow.[17]

By 'tomorrow' he is referring to the future, and the contestation of the future is clear through his struggle with the farmer. To ensure that the labour tenants do not have any claim to the land, the farmers are going as far as destroying the land.

Another tactic employed by those that lease the farm, as explained by Mr Mahlangu, seems to be that they want to kill the cattle belonging to the labour tenants. 'Today I and my family do not have any water to drink. It has been more than three weeks now and sometimes we go up to two months without water. They want to kill my cows. They want to kill me.'[18] In African culture, the death of a cow is the death of one's future.

Despite all of these challenges, the labour tenants continue to stay on the farms and they do so because the land is where their parents are buried and they also want to be buried there. In my PhD thesis, in looking at farmworkers in Gauteng who had no title deeds, I argued that this question of death was an eschatological anxiety, reflected as the question, 'Where will we die?'[19] For the labour tenants in Bethal the answer is, 'In this land where our parents are buried. That is where we will die.' This is an eschatological gaze: the labour tenants' eyes see the land as a place of birth and death.

When speaking today of the colonial encounter in South Africa, it is clear in the public discourse that landlessness is at the core of the historical injustice that Black people have suffered. Mr Mazibuko was aware that there were talks about the land being returned to its rightful owners (expropriation without compensation):

> I am staying on the farm because I am hoping that one day we will wake up and be told that here is your future and you can share it with your children. If this does not happen, maybe I can consider going to the township. But, I have cattle that need land to graze and water to drink. Here on the farm, we are faced with water challenges and sometimes it is unbearable and I begin to entertain the idea of going to the township. But then again, I hope for a better future in this land because my father is buried here and we had planned for my mother to be buried here as well.[20]

The existence of family graves on the farm links those that remain on the farm with their ancestors and serves as concrete evidence that they belong to the farm. The living conditions have become difficult for many, and most labour tenants feel that it is the intention of the new farmers who lease or buy the land to push them off the farm so that they do not make any claims about belonging there. This is the futurity of violence: once violence is used, it does not want the future to be contested. The existence of the labour tenants on the farm means that they will contest the future by referring to the past and even pointing to the graves as their proof of belonging to the farm. Mr Mazibuko adds: 'They prefer us in the townships, so that they say go back to the township where you belong. You do not stay on this farm. You only work here so you do not belong here!'[21]

'A white man was a white man'

The white society in South Africa is also in a state of ontological anxiety. This is reflected in its claim to the vast land in a country where they are a minority. Violence conceals the anxiety of the white farmer, but also reveals the nature of private property as that which is protected through violence so that the future is not contested. The farmers in Bethal were seeing their future and aiming to create a docile being who would not contest it. This anxiety about the future also expressed itself through the violent nationalist project known as apartheid, which promoted the idea of the superiority of the white race. Violence was used so that whites' authority on the farm was not challenged; in so doing, farmers were ensuring that in the future those who work for them will not challenge them. This is what Mr Mavuso called a 'white man being a white man'.[22] That is to say, apartheid on the farm and outside the farm ensured that white society did not get challenged in any way. Mr Mavuso continued:

During apartheid the white man was a white man. Today things are changing. You can call them by their name; during apartheid you would never call a white person by name. If you had done something that is not right you were going to be punished. Even if you knew that you could hit them back, you would not be able to. They have dogs and other workers to assist them. You would never do anything ... The reason I stopped working on this farm was because the farmer's son after finishing school attempted to hit me. He tried taking chances and wanted to hit me and I said no ... you will not try that with me. I stopped working for them and then went to work on another farm.[23]

To resist violence was to take on a positive image of the self as an individual who refused to be treated like a docile being. However, as Mr Mavuso knew, the refusal meant that he could not work on the farm anymore and that was why he decided to go and work elsewhere. The farmer was the law: challenging the farmer meant that one no longer belonged on the farm. To challenge the farmer was to jeopardise one's future on the farm. Even when the farmer allowed for workers to retaliate in a fight, their future was still uncertain. Mr Mazibuko told an interesting story:

> Prior to 1980 [the time he started working on the farm] ... we were told that the farmer allowed for workers to fight him. With his children, the ones I worked for, that was not allowed. The old man allowed for a worker to fight him one on one. He would say when he is hitting you, if you can, also hit back. He was strong, but with his children they hit you but you do not retaliate. He allowed for the worker to fight back because he knew he was stronger ... There are workers who were able to win a fight, but the problem is that after that they never knew if he had a grudge against them. He did not show that he had any grudge. But, because in your head, you are aware that you have hit a white farmer, then let me just leave the farm. There are three individual workers who won the face to face fight against him, but after the victory they decided to leave the farm. Since they never knew what would happen to them in the future.[24]

When looking at the use of violence today, all labour tenants indicated that the farmers did not hit them anymore, because they knew that under democracy workers had rights and could have them arrested. However, farmers used other forms of coercion to push workers off the land. Mr Mazibuko's opinion was that farmers are threatened by all these rights:

> The house that I am staying in ... we are fighting for it. The farmer wants me out because I no longer work for them. I went to the local councillor, and he went to speak to the farmer and came back and told me that I can continue staying in this house. As I said, I have been here for many years ... Even the grave of my father can prove that.[25]

Those who use violence are not driven only by cupidity; they also seek to remove any claim of belonging from those who work the land. The farmer is aware that to work the land is to have a relationship with it, to understand and obey its rhythm and to give in to its beauty. In my interview with the farmer who owns Legdaar, he told me that his family has been on the farm for more than three generations. One thing that he has always loved about farming, he said, 'is the smell of the harvest ... that smell is the smell of the land. I can't describe how it makes me feel. As I think about it, it raises my hair.'[26] It is the smell of belonging, but it is not a smell of equality to the farmer.

This is linked to dispossession. In the making of private property, the Black people were removed from the land, then brought back to work on it and, in the language of paternalism, were said to be children belonging to the farmer. Today this is challenged. But the difficult thing for the white farmers is that the workers point and say, 'Look over there. That is where my parents' grave is and this is where I will be returned.'

The legal experts will point to the importance of the Extension of Security of Tenure Act 62 of 1997, chapter IV, on the termination of the right of residence and eviction:

> 8(4) The right of residence of an occupier who has resided on the land in question or any other land belonging to the owner for 10 years and – (a) has reached the age of 60 years; or (b) is an employee

or former employee of the owner or person in charge, and as a result of ill health, injury or disability is unable to supply labour to the owner or person in charge, may not be terminated unless that occupier has committed a breach contemplated in section 10(1) (a), (b) or (c): Provided that for the purposes of this subsection, the mere refusal or failure to provide labour shall not constitute such a breach.[27]

Despite being on the farm for more than 10 years and able to point to their parents' graves, and having an awareness that they belong to the land, all the labour tenants indicated that they do not have any legal documents that validate their occupancy. Although the white man is being challenged today, on the farm he remains the law. Consider what is happening at Bleskbokspruit and Legdaar farms as relayed in Mr Mazibuko's words: 'I am still fighting for this house and do not know what will happen in the future. We as farmworkers are isolated from the cities and our problems are not easy to see.'[28] That is the limit of the law, that not everyone has access to the eyes that will see and assist, the eyes of lawyers or political authorities.[29] There is no written contract, no date of occupancy, only a grave that belongs to the parents who used to work on the farm. The farmers continue to be the law; if they no longer want the tenants, they can easily evict them. The children, as Mr Mathebe indicated, cannot tolerate this ontological nowhereness. They leave the farm, yet they go to nowhere, to the township.

'The ancestors are left to see for themselves'
Those who leave the farm leave behind not only their parents but also their ancestors. This point was also made by Mr Magwaza:

> This is life today here on the farm. We are poor and the elderly are left with their children who have no work on the farm. We are seeing the coming of coal mines and hope that maybe our children will be employed in them. But as you can see many of the young

have left the farm … they have left the graves of their ancestors. Those graves are not taken care of. The ancestors are left to see for themselves … Unfortunately, you cannot run away from your ancestors. In the future they will call you even in your dreams. To come to make life better at home.[30]

Mr Magwaza is seeing his future as an ancestor, that when he himself is amongst his ancestors his grave will not be taken care of. On the farm, those that are insistently holding on are awaiting their death while confronting death (the violence of dispossession). They are waiting to be returned to the land they were born on. Some of the children cannot take this hardship that their parents are faced with; they, too, confront ontological nowhereness. Mr Magwaza's last remarks point to the eschatological future, indicating that the link to the land is spiritual; therefore, those who think they have escaped the hardship, and have left their ancestors to take care of themselves, must know that their ancestors will call them one day to return. There is no escaping the land – that is our eschatological future – and today the 'land' is on everyone's tongue. That is the call of all the ancestors who fell on this land, calling to those in distant cities to return to them. There are no peaceful dreams, we learn, for those who have left their ancestors behind. Even in the city they will be confronted by what they said they were running away from. As Mr Mathebe said, in the city they do not have homes and do not even have a claim to a grave. That is the eschatological future of South Africa. It is indeed a cause of anxiety. The elderly in Bethal are confronting it, while some of the young are running away from it – but they will be called back. It seems that there is no escaping this home, this land, with its violence, and with the calls for those who flee to 'come to make life better at home'.

Chapter 7 | Our eschatological future

There are people who are like tigers thirsting for blood. Anyone who
has once experienced this power, this unlimited mastery of the body,
blood and soul of a fellow man made of the same clay as himself, a
brother in the law of Christ, anyone who has experienced the power
and full licence to inflict the greatest humiliation upon another crea-
ture made in the image of God will unconsciously lose the mastery
of his own sensations. Tyranny is a habit; it may develop, and it does
develop at last, into a disease. — Fyodor Dostoevsky[1]

The creation of large hectares of farmland in South Africa involved
the brutal annihilation of people not considered human. Fyodor
Dostoevsky argues that anyone who has killed will lose mastery of their
sensations, and I have argued that they will have iqunga, which is an
urge to continue to kill. In focusing on Bethal, I linked the history of
dispossession to how the white society in South Africa was suffering
from anxiety related to how they deprived Black people of their land.
Dispossession is not a complete act since the dispossessor fears that
those who get removed from the land will contest it in future. That is
the futurity of violence – it aims to ensure that the future of land is not
contested. This futurity is embedded in the problem of ontology; philo-
sophically, ontology, or being in the world, is claiming the self through
violence. The claim of the self is about being recognised by the Other

through the use of violence, 'through a life-and-death struggle'.[2] This is the insatiability of violence in ontology.

Through looking at dispossession, I have, firstly, argued that Black people had to confront ontological nowhereness, which is about dealing with the state of being homeless. The state of being homeless is related to how the white society claimed its being in the world – that white people are superior. I showed the limits of this superiority in that it has to confront the unknown future. My argument is that the violence of ontology in white society reflects their anxiety about the future. In positing that dispossession impacted both Black and white people as an ontological problem, I aimed to show the limits of ontological violence. To use violence to stake one's existence in the world means that through the killing of the Other, killers do not always become the master of their selves (they will have iqunga or will always be haunted by the unknown future/spirit of those they killed).

Secondly, I have shown what being on the land was like for Black people and how they had to create possibilities of finding a home, without the use of violence, to be recognised as humans. I have asserted that this was an eschatological problem, about the future of the spirits of the dispossessed. In looking at Bethal, I have argued that violence did not achieve its goal since those who died remained on the land and were resurrected; they came back looking like potatoes. The potatoes that looked like humans showed how the land carried within it a spiritual encounter – an encounter with spirits that refused to be forgotten and demanded justice. Thus, Bethal was haunted not only by ghosts of the past but by ghosts of a historical present as well. This historical present represents how dispossession in South Africa is linked with the body and the soul of the dispossessed. This is our eschatological future; it confronts us every day in South Africa. Even the ancestors are fighting for the land: they haunt the present to resolve the past. The potato that looked like a human served as a reminder of the unresolved future of the land. It was a call for justice in South Africa for all the dispossessed working on the land without the land.

In using the eye as a heuristic model, I have shown that not every-thing is visible in this land. The story of the dead buried in the land provides us with an archaeological reference point which reveals that, during a particular historical period in South Africa, there were people who worked the land and were interred like dogs. They had no other place to run to because the farm where they laboured was their home, their future. Using this heuristic model, I focused on different eyes look-ing at the future of the land in South Africa: the eyes of the farmer, the labourer, the state and the liberal activist. Through these eyes, I began to delve more deeply into the meaning of land. My argument is that Bethal is always present, whenever there are humans on the land, working the land, seeking to live and make life. The making of life on the land and the return of life to the land is part of the eschatological future. The eschatological future is not just about the return of the question of the land in the public domain, as we have witnessed in the last decade in South Africa, but more about the ever-present relationship of the body and the land, belonging and death. This spiritual future always refers us to the past. As we discuss land expropriation without compensation, there is a need to look into the meaning of land beyond its material value.

This land is home

In looking at the history of dispossession, Solomon Plaatje showed that the 1913 Land Act reflected the spiritual problem facing white and Black people in South Africa. He showed that life begins from the land as the home and the source of spiritual existence. However, the white society made Black people pariahs of nowhere. In their state of nowhereness, Black people did not give up hope that one day they would return to their home, the land. This was not only an ontological contestation, which involved creating a new state of being in this condition of nowhereness, but a refusal for the spirit to be homeless. The home was positioned as a future spiritual goal. Plaatje wrote:

We are told to forgive our enemies and not to let the sun go down upon our wrath, so we breathe the prayer that peace may be to the white races ... In the beginning, we are told, God created heaven and earth, and peopled the earth, for people do not shoot up to heaven from nowhere. They must have had an earthly home. Enoch, Melchizedek, Elijah, and other saints, came to heaven from earth. God did not say to the Israelites in their bondage: 'Cheer up, boys; bear it all in good part for I have bright mansions on high awaiting you all.' But he said: 'I have surely seen the affliction of my people which are in Egypt, and have heard their cry by reason of their taskmasters; for I know their sorrows, and I am come down to bring them out of the hands of the Egyptians, and to bring them up out of that land unto a good land and a large, unto a land flowing with milk and honey.'[3]

In South Africa, the worker and the farmer do not differ that much in how they see the land. Both see it as their home. Through the historical fact of dispossession, this land remains contested and both parties are aware of it.[4] The farmer looks at the workers as potential usurpers and the workers look at the farmer as a thief. Farmworkers in Bethal cannot imagine life away from the farm even though they are reminded by the farmer that they do not own the land (or belong in this land). The condition of ontological nowhereness in democratic South Africa is visible in how most workers, despite being on the farm for decades, still have no security of tenure. This condition of ontological nowhereness of the Black person continues to create anxiety amongst the white farming community that one day they will be like the Black person, removed from the land. This anxiety about the future led to the violence on the farms and resulted in the formation of the apartheid state, which aimed to protect the white society from the unknown future. This unknown future was a rejection of being governed by a Black government. Today this future has come to pass. Black people are in government. The white farming community is already talking about genocide, a future where Black people kill all white South Africans.

Today, the white farming community argues that democratic South Africa is a violent state that does not care about them. They use the term 'genocide' to refer to the crimes that happen on the farms that involve the robbing and brutal killing of farmers. White farmers looking from the past would argue that this was the future they were trying to prevent by ensuring that the Black person remained docile. The reference to white genocide speaks directly to the future – that at this pace, in the future the minority in South Africa will not exist. In looking at the relations on most South African farms, we see that they continue to be violent; the farmer continues to be the law. However, the law does not go unchallenged. As in the past, the challenge on South African farms is not about changing the attitudes of white farmers so that they treat their workers better. This recommendation misses the contestation that happens on the farms, which is linked to the future of the land in this country. Every form of anxiety reveals and also conceals. What is revealed in looking at this anxiety is that the future is unstable. What is concealed is that the violence on the farms is linked to the history of dispossession.

On 30 October 2017, the white farming community staged what is known as the Black Monday protest. The protest saw farmers from different provinces in South Africa demanding protection from the state. Some of the placards they held were written in Afrikaans, with slogans like 'Genoeg is genoeg' (Enough is enough). The protest was directed at the failure of the Black-led state to protect the white farmers. The desire to return to the previous apartheid state was seen in how some of those farmers carried the old apartheid flag (in use from 1928 to 1994), which includes emblems of the Union Jack, the Orange Free State and the South African Republic. The flag of the past was brought to the present to remind the white farming community of the protection they had lost. The symbol of the past is used in the present to threaten the Black people. Therefore, when the flag is waved in the present, it serves to remind Black people what the white society is capable of.

In looking at Bethal and through my academic research in agriculture over the last decade, I have come to an awareness that the farm as a hidden space continues to conceal violence that is masked as the paternalism of the farmer. The paternal discourse presents the white farmer as a benevolent father who cares for his children, the farmworkers. Paternalism denies seeing Black adults as independent human beings who can make their own decisions. To discipline the 'child', violence is used. Is it any wonder that people subjected to violence for many years respond violently? In visiting Bethal today, I encountered labour tenants such as Mr Mazibuko, who said he would continue to stay on the farm despite having to struggle for tenancy, because he hoped that in future the land would return to the workers (using the language of expropriation without compensation).

The eschatological future

In my first encounter with the stories in Bethal, I wondered what kind of human being brings so much terror and fear to the eyes of the Other. Do they do it out of pleasure, or are they also victims of trauma and forced by that trauma to enjoy it because it makes them larger than life, because they have a right over another life? Every act of violence carries consequences; it never leaves the agents of that violence the same, for they have seen the face of the Other and decided to subject it to an ontological terror of violence. This terror is ontological, for ontology is related to claiming one's existence through violence. Those who do not retaliate through violence are in the space of nothingness or invisibility. Violence can be transcended as soon as the eye encounters the face of the Other. If we see the face of the Other, we see their spirit, and seeing their spirit is to heed the demand of not committing murder. But we must remember that the eye is not innocent; it is an organ of prejudice, shaped by its time. In the period covered in this book, the face of this Other carried no meaning, for they were beings suffering from ontological nowhereness in the country of their birth. This search for a home rendered them creatures of nowhere by the eye that inflicts violence and terror. The white society found comfort in arguing that they were not dealing with humans with individual faces but with a threat.

That is where the ethics of the eye reaches its limits. I am now walking in contradistinction to the proposition by Levinas[5] since we shall always find the 'eye' guilty by judging it from our time. The guilt of the eye was made apparent by the potato since it ridiculed the entire white farming community for the violence it committed against the workers. The potato that looked like a human was about the future because, to the public, the violence in Bethal came to be about justice for the violated workers on South African farms. Therefore, Bethal was an exposé of hidden practices, not only in the farming community in Mpumalanga, but in agriculture throughout South Africa. I was already in the future when I was conversing with the children of the labour tenants and hearing how they experienced violence on the farms in Bethal. Just like their parents, they are subjected to the terror of being reminded that this 'home', the farm, is not their home since they do not have the title deed. Just like their parents, they are resilient and continue to resist being pushed out, but their own children, as we have seen, are fleeing the farms to live a life in the city without any anchor to the 'home'. The parents look with pity at the generation of children that run away from the conditions at home because they know that soon, one way or another, they will have to confront their nowhereness and somehow resolve it.

This is not a conclusion

This chapter is not a conclusion but a beginning of the retelling of the historical present concerning the land question in South Africa. To conclude means to put an end to the struggles of the dead, to bury a spectre whose haunting we could put a halt to in our present. The spectre returns today in the form of the land expropriation debate to remind us of the unjust historical past, which is unresolved on South Africa's farms. This moment even revealed itself to the sangoma in the call to free the dead who were buried like dogs (see chapter 2). The demand from the dead for freedom reminds us that justice in the present cannot be complete unless the spirits of the dead are set free. This book forms part of documenting the contested meaning of the future of the land in South Africa. However, this final chapter is not a conclusion but a confrontation with resurrection, because I have resurrected the struggles of the dead in a particular moment in South African history. In looking through the eyes of the dead, the ailment of our spirit becomes apparent. We are all confronted by death but none of us is sure of the day it will strike. In this return to the past, we encountered a people who fled from a death-bound life created by dispossession to a life of ubiquitous death[6] created on a farm. There is a sort of resistance, for they saw death wearing the face of a violent farmer, a violent white society that did not recognise them as belonging to humanity or society. On the farm, they looked death in the eyes with one single flame of passion burning in their hearts: the knowledge that this deplorable state of existence was their home. There is never a perfect home; indeed, imperfections are part of what makes a house a home. Home is not just a spiritual entity of great-grandparents found buried in the land so that one can be returned to them, as one was introduced to them through the umbilical cord at birth.

My eyes have seen the future and its echoes of destiny, hope and family. This is a future where the cattle continue to remind us of a distant horizon that remains forever present, ephemeral suffering, for the future is always a product of joy. Bethal of yesterday no longer exists. Bethal of today cannot speak of yesterday. What I found in Bethal in the present was a negation of forms of narration of the past, revealing that there was never a happy past and that sorrow remains present in our soul (the land). The soul transcends time; this is the eschatological gift. This is a gift of life created in an encounter with death to make a home for the future. Those that see a home or make a home know that in the process of creation, there is never a state of joy for those that make a home since they create to transcend suffering for the coming generation, a generation that might flee what the parents have created for them. Unfortunately, they cannot escape home. Home is a spiritual gift, which is why to see the land is to see its spirit, and the potato that came back looking like a human reminds us of this connection between the body, land, home and the spirit. This is the identity and script of any human being, which is to say, one is born somewhere and, in death, one returns to the land. Bethal remains forever present as long as there is a labourer, vast hectares of land and a desire to make a home in such conditions.

Notes

Prologue: Emazambaneni: The land of terror

1   Letter (author not identified) written from Leslie jail, Bethal, to head of prisons department, Pretoria, and shared by William Barney Ngakane with Henri-Philippe Junod, national organiser of the Penal Reform League, in a letter dated 15 March 1954, AD 1947/25.3, Historical Papers Research Archive, University of the Witwatersrand, Johannesburg (hereafter cited as Historical Papers Research Archive).

2   William Shakespeare, *Julius Caesar,* act I, scene 2, lines 52–53.

3   uMbuso weNkosi, in conversation with Mam Winnie, 9 December 2017.

4   Ralph Ellison, *Invisible Man* (London: Penguin Classics, 1952), 316.

5   William Edward Burghardt Du Bois, *Black Reconstruction in America 1860– 1880: An Essay Toward a History of the Part which Black Folk Played in the Attempt to Reconstruct Democracy in America* (Cleveland and New York: World Publishing Company, 1935), 714.

6   Hortense J. Spillers, 'Mama's Baby, Papa's Maybe: An American Grammar Book', in 'Culture and Countermemory: The "American" Connection', special issue, *Diacritics* 17, no. 2 (Summer 1987): 76.

7   Jacques Derrida, 'Archive Fever: A Freudian Impression', *Diacritics* 25, no. 2 (Summer 1995): 55.

8   Here I have in my head a song by Notorious B.I.G., 'You're Nobody til Somebody Kills You'.

9   Emmanuel Levinas, *Totality and Infinity: An Essay on Exteriority* (The Hague: Nijhoff Publishers, 1969), 21.

10 Linda T. Smith, *Decolonizing Methodologies: Research and Indigenous Peoples* (London: Zed Books, 1999).

11 Walter Benjamin, *Reflections: Essays, Aphorisms, Autobiographical Writing* (New York: Schocken Books, 1986), 295.

12 Cheryl Walker and Ben Cousins, 'Land Divided, Land Restored: Introduction', in *Land Divided Land Restored: Land Reform in South Africa for the 21st Century*, ed. Ben Cousins and Cheryl Walker (Johannesburg: Jacana Media, 2015), 4.

13 Emile Durkheim, *The Division of Labour in Society* (London: Macmillan Press, 1984), 43.

14 Walter Benjamin notes: 'For the function of violence in lawmaking is two-fold, in the sense that lawmaking pursues as its end, with violence as the means, what is to be established as law, but at the moment of instatement does not dismiss violence; rather, at this very moment of lawmaking, it specifically established as law not an end unalloyed by violence, but one necessarily and intimately bound to it, under the title of power. Lawmaking is power making, and, to that extent, an immediate manifestation of violence' (Benjamin, *Reflections*, 295). Instead of only seeing violence as law-making and law-making as power making, I take a Durkheimian view by adding crime in relation to violence and I argue that violence and law reflect the social order. To go beyond Durkheim (*The Division of Labour in Society*) and Benjamin (*Reflections*), I added into the formulation the issue of the unknown future as that which destabilises the project of violence as law-making. Because the future is unknown, it creates anxiety in every social order.

15 Durkheim, *The Division of Labour in Society*, 43; Benjamin, *Reflections*, 262.

Chapter 1: The spectre of the human potato

1 Mr Ngubeza Mahlangu, interviewed by Tshepo Moloi, eMzinoni, Bethal, 4 August 2008.

2 Thomas Karis and Gail M. Gerhart, eds., *Challenge and Violence 1953–1964*, vol. 3 of *From Protest to Challenge: A Documentary History of African Politics in South Africa 1882–1964*, ed. Thomas G. Karis and Gail M. Gerhart (Stanford, CA: Hoover Institution Press, 1977), 292.

3 Mandla Nkosi, 'Why Potato Boycott was Called Off', *New Age*, 10 September 1959, 1.

4 Mr Soko, interviewed by uMbuso weNkosi, eMzinoni, Bethal, 26 January 2020.

5 See Michael Scott, 'Memorandum on Compound Labour Conditions in Agriculture, Bethal District', 1947, AB684f, Historical Papers Research Archive; Ruth First, 'Bethal Case-Book', *Africa South* 2, no. 3 (1958); Ruth First, 'Exposure! The Farm Labour Scandal', *New Age* pamphlet, 1959; Henry Nxumalo, 'Bethal Today: *Drum's* Fearless Exposure of Human Exploitation',

Drum magazine, April 1952; William Barney Ngakane, 'Report of Inquiry into the Working Conditions of Prison Farm Labourers', South African Institute of Race Relations, AD 1947/25.3, Historical Papers Research Archive.

6   Deborah Posel, *The Making of Apartheid 1948–1961: Conflict and Compromise* (Oxford: Clarendon Press, 1991), 139.

7   Reported by Henry Nxumalo in 'Bethal Today', 4.

8   Adam Ashforth, 'On the Native Question: A Reading of the Grand Tradition of Commissions of Inquiry into the "Native Question" in Twentieth-Century South Africa' (PhD thesis, Oxford University, 1987), 55.

9   Frances Baard, *My Spirit Is Not Banned* (Harare: Zimbabwe Publishing House, 1986), https://www.sahistory.org.za/archive/dont-eat-potatoes, accessed 1 December 2021.

10 Billy Nair, 'Through the Eyes of the Workers', in *Reflections in Prison: Voices from the South African Liberation Struggle*, ed. Mac Maharaj (Amherst and Boston: University of Massachusetts Press, 2001), 170.

11 Nicky Rousseau, 'The Farm, the River and the Picnic Spot: Topographies of Terror', *African Studies* 68, no. 3 (2009): 354.

12 This was a military strategy that involved burning anything that might help the Boer commandos who were fighting the British army. Houses and farms of civilians were burned because they provided food to the Boer commandos. See Liz Stanley, *Mourning Becomes ... Post/memory, Commemoration and the Concentration Camps of the South African War* (Johannesburg: Wits University Press, 2008), 5.

13 John Higginson, *Collective Violence and the Agrarian Origins of South African Apartheid* (New York: Cambridge University Press, 2015), 21.

14 Stanley, *Mourning Becomes*, 3.

15 Leonard Monteath Thompson, *The Unification of South Africa, 1902–1910* (Oxford: Clarendon Press, 1960), 20; Nigel Worden, *The Making of Modern South Africa: Conquest, Apartheid, Democracy* (Chichester: Wiley-Blackwell, 2012), 15–16; Paul Rich, 'Segregation and the Cape Liberal Tradition', Collected Seminar Papers, Institute of Commonwealth Studies 26 (1981).

16 Rosalynde Ainslie, *Masters and Serfs: Farm Labour in South Africa* (London: International Defence and Aid Fund for Southern Africa, 1977), 7.

17 Solomon Plaatje, *Native Life in South Africa, Before and Since the European War and the Boer Rebellion* (Urbana, IL: Project Gutenberg, 1998), 15.

18 Plaatje, *Native Life in South Africa*, 63.

19 Emmanuel Levinas, *Alterity and Transcendence* (London: Athlone Press, 1999), 4–7; Emmanuel Levinas, *Otherwise than Being or Beyond Essence*, trans. Alphonso Lingis (The Hague: Nijhoff Publishers, 1974), 181–182; Jacques Derrida, *The Gift of Death* (Chicago: University of Chicago Press, 1995), 3–5.

20 Lauren Segal, *A Brutal Harvest: The Roots and Legitimation of Violence on Farms in South Africa* (Johannesburg: Black Sash, 1991); Africa Check, 'Report of the Committee of Inquiry into Farm Attacks', 31 July 2003, https://africacheck. org/sites/default/files/Final-Report-Committee-of-Inquiry-Farm-Attacks-July-2003.pdf, accessed 2 December 2015.

21 Andries du Toit, 'Paternalism and Modernity on South African Wine and Fruit Farms: An Analysis of Paternalist Constructions of Community and Authority in the Discourse of Coloured Farm Workers in the Stellenbosch Region' (PhD thesis, University of Essex, 1996), 53–55.

22 Du Toit, 'Paternalism and Modernity on South African Wine and Fruit Farms', 55.

23 Charles van Onselen, 'The Social and Economic Underpinning of Paternalism and Violence on the Maize Farms of the South-Western Transvaal, 1900–1950', *Journal of Historical Sociology* 5, no. 2 (June 1992); Cornelius William de Kiewiet, *A History of South Africa: Social and Economic* (London: Oxford University Press, 1941), 56; Helen Bradford, *A Taste of Freedom: The ICU in Rural South Africa, 1924–1930* (Johannesburg: Ravan Press, 1988), 13–20.

24 Levinas, *Otherwise than Being or Beyond Essence*, 271.

25 Salaman Redcliffe, *The History and Social Influence of the Potato* (Cambridge: Cambridge University Press, 1949).

Chapter 2: Whose eyes are looking at history?

1 Plaatje, *Native Life in South Africa*, 59–60.

2 See Mbuso Nkosi, 'Doing Research Otherwise: Critical Essays on "the Land Question", Farmworkers and Resistance in South Africa' (PhD thesis, University of the Witwatersrand, 2018).

3 Michel Foucault, *The History of Sexuality*, vol. 1, *An Introduction* (New York: Pantheon Books, 1978), 118–119.

4 Sihle Manda, 'Tortured Souls of Dududu', *IOL*, 24 March 2015, http://www.iol.co.za/news/south-africa/kwazulu-natal/tortured-souls-of-dududu-1836293, accessed 4 April 2016.

5 Amanda Khoza, 'Sangoma Tells How She Located KZN Graves', *The Witness*, 24 March 2015, https://www.news24.com/SouthAfrica/News/

Sangoma-tells-how-she-located-KZN-graves-20150324, accessed 4 April 2016.

6   Manda, 'Tortured Souls of Dududu'.

7   Manda, 'Tortured Souls of Dududu'.

8   Bongani Mthethwa, Matthew Savides and Taschica Pillay, 'Unearthing the Secrets of KwaZulu-Natal's Farm of Horrors', *TimesLive*, 27 March 2015, https://www.timeslive.co.za/news/south-africa/2015-03-27-unearthing-the-secrets-of-kwazulu-natals-farm-of-horrors/, accessed 4 April 2016.

9   Bongani Mthethwa et al., 'Unearthing the Secrets of KwaZulu-Natal's Farm of Horrors'.

10   Timothy Moloke, Letter to the South African Institute of Race Relations, 23 May 1953, AD 1947/25.1.2, Farm Labour General Correspondence 1951–1953, Historical Papers Research Archive.

11   Scott, 'Memorandum on Compound Labour Conditions', 4.

12   Bevis Fairbrother, 'My Take: Politicians Now CSI Experts?' *South Coast Herald*, 28 March 2015, https://southcoastherald.co.za/81596/my-take-politicians-now-csi-experts/, accessed 4 April 2016.

13   Kamcilla Pillay and Nosipho Mngoma, 'Mass Graves Found on KZN Farm', *IOL*, 16 March 2015, https://www.iol.co.za/news/crime-courts/mass-graves-found-on-kzn-farm-1832544, accessed 4 April 2016.

14   When I contacted Klatzow, who now resides in the United Kingdom, tele-phonically on 15 March 2021, he said he had forgotten about the case and had sold his practice and that 'six years is a long time ago'. This came as a shock to me given his 'frozen in time' statement.

15   Frederick van Wyk and William Barney Ngakane, 'Pass Offenders and Farm Labour', 21 September 1949, AD 1947/25.2, Historical Papers Research Archive.

16   Van Wyk and Ngakane, 'Pass Offenders and Farm Labour'.

17   A. Hoedemaker, Letters to Frederick van Wyk (acting director of South African Institute of Race Relations), 24 March 1952; 2 April 1952; AD 1947/25.1.2, Farm Labour General Correspondence 1951–1953, Historical Papers Research Archive.

18   Hoedemaker, Letters.

19   Frederick J. van Wyk, Letters to Mrs A. Hoedemaker, 3 March 1952; 19 May 1952; AD 1947/25.1.2, Farm Labour General Correspondence 1951–1953, Historical Papers Research Archive.

20   Van Wyk, Letters to Mrs A. Hoedemaker.

21   Timothy Mitchell, *Colonising Egypt* (Berkeley: University of California Press, 1991), xvi. Mitchell argues that it was not a mistake that this metaphysics of representation referred back to Europe, since it was in Europe that the colonised world was presented as lacking order and truth.

22   A farmer I interviewed in 2021, who was farming in the 1970s, after the scandal, said with pride that 'prisoners loved working in the farms because they were given food and had access to open land'. Mr Groebler, interviewed by uMbuso weNkosi and Xender Ehlers, Bethal, 15 October 2021.

23   *Rand Daily Mail*, 'Bethal Farmers Vindicated, Says Lawrence: Allegations of Widespread Abuses Unfounded', 21 July 1947.

24   *Rand Daily Mail*, 'Bethal Farmers Vindicated, Says Lawrence'.

25   Anne Yates and Lewis Chester, *The Troublemaker: Michael Scott and His Lonely Struggle Against Injustice* (London: Aurum Press, 2006), 71–72.

26   Yates and Chester, *The Troublemaker*, 72.

27   Scott, 'Memorandum on Compound Labour Conditions', 5–8.

28   *Sunday Times*, 'Farm Labour: Another Body Exhumed', 21 June 1959.

29   *Rand Daily Mail*, 'Inquest Told of Farm Labourer's Beating', 9 July 1959.

30   In decolonial theory, scholars refer to Walter Mignolo on the locus of enunciation in reference to how seeing, feeling and thinking are shaped by power and politics. Walter D. Mignolo, 'Epistemic Disobedience, Independent Thought and De-Colonial Freedom', *Theory, Culture & Society* 26, no. 7–8 (2009).

Chapter 3: Bethal, the house of God

1   Genesis 28:16–17 (NIV), https://www.biblegateway.com/passage/?search=Genesis%2028%3A10-18&version=NIV, accessed 10 January 2023.

2   Transvaal Government Gazette, no. 213, Tuesday, 12 October 1880, Historical Papers Research Archive.

3   G.P. Bothma, W.A. de Klerk, C.B. Ehlers and J.H. van Niekerk, 'Bethal 1880–1980 – Eeufees Gedenkalbum', Bethal Stadsraad, Bethal, 1980.

4   Bothma et al., 'Bethal 1880–1980'.

5   Stanley, *Mourning Becomes*, 5.

6   Stanley, *Mourning Becomes*, 101–120.

7   Martin Murray, 'Factories in the Fields: Capitalist Farming in the Bethal District, 1910–1950', in *White Farms, Black Labor: The State and Agrarian Change in Southern Africa*, ed. Alan Jeeves and Jonathan Crush (Portsmouth: Heinemann, 1997), 83.

8   Taylorism, or scientific management, is attributed to Frederick Winslow Taylor, author of *The Principles of Scientific Management* (New York: Harper & Brothers, 1947). Taylor describes a scientific method by which management can make the labour process more efficient by breaking down work into simple, repetitive tasks; building on the capabilities of workers; and monitoring worker performance.

9   Murray, 'Factories in the Fields'.

10 A reference to Jesus' words in John 14:2 (NIV): 'My father's house has many rooms ... I am going there to prepare a place for you', https://www.biblegateway.com/passage/?search=John%2014%3A2&version=NIV, accessed 13 March 2023.

11 Matthew 19:24 (NIV), https://www.biblegateway.com/passage/?search=Matthew%2019%3A24&version=NIV, accessed 1 March 2023.

12 First, 'Bethal Case-Book', 14–25; see also First, 'Exposure! The Farm Labour Scandal'.

13 First, 'Bethal Case-Book', 18.

14 First, 'Bethal Case-Book', 14.

15 Scott, 'Memorandum on Compound Labour Conditions', 17.

16 Scott, 'Memorandum on Compound Labour Conditions', 1.

17 Murray, 'Factories in the Fields', 92.

18 *Rand Daily Mail*, 'Bethal an Ideal Holiday Resort and Residential Centre', 25 May 1936.

19 *Rand Daily Mail*, 'Bethal Famers Vindicated, Says Lawrence'.

20 First, 'Bethal Case-Book', 25.

21 See Assistant Director of Native Agriculture in Flagstaff, Re: Training of Natives in Agricultural Colleges, Letter to Quintin Whyte, 19 July 1948, AD 1947/25.1.1, General Correspondence from 1947–1950, Historical Papers Research Archive.

22 Nxumalo, 'Bethal Today', 7.

23 Nxumalo, 'Bethal Today', 7.

24 National Organiser of the Penal Reform League of South Africa, Letter addressed to the Director of Prisons in Cape Town, 12 May 1952, AD 1947/25.3, Historical Papers Research Archive.

25 This is well covered in Patrick Duncan, *South Africa's Rule of Violence* (London: Methuen, 1964).

26 Scott, 'Memorandum on Compound Labour Conditions', 17.

27 Scott, 'Memorandum on Compound Labour Conditions', 17.

28 Anthony Sampson, *Drum: A Venture into the New Africa* (London: Collins, 1956), 49.

29 Jürgen Schadeberg, *The Way I See It: A Memoir* (Johannesburg: Picador Africa, 2017), 172–173.

30 Marian Lacey, *Working for Boroko: The Origins of a Coercive Labour System in South Africa* (Johannesburg: Ravan Press, 1981), 138.

31 Lacey, *Working for Boroko*, 141.

32 See Edith Rheinallt Jones, 'Farm Labour in the Transvaal', *Race Relations Journal* 12, no. 1, 1945, AD 1947/25.5, Historical Papers Research Archive.

33 First, 'Bethal Case-Book', 18.

34 National Organiser of the Penal Reform League of South Africa, Letter.

35 Ms Elizabeth Mkhwanazi, interviewed by Tshepo Moloi, eMzinoni, Bethal, 20 August 2008; Mr Mavumeni John Nsibande, interviewed by Tshepo Moloi, eMzinoni, Bethal, 21 August 2008.

36 Mr Soko, interview.

37 Hansard, no. 20-16/6/59, col. 8202-8203, AD 1947/25.4, Historical Papers Research Archive.

38 Hansard.

39 Nxumalo, 'Bethal Today', 8.

40 Sampson, *Drum*, 38.

41 *Rand Daily Mail*, 'Three Farm Foremen Fined', 21 July 1947.

42 *Rand Daily Mail*, 'Farmer Fined for Beating Convicts', 28 May 1959.

43 Ngakane, 'Report of Inquiry into the Working Conditions of Prison Farm Labourers'.

44 Henry Nxumalo, 'Mr Drum Looks at the Tot System', *Drum* magazine, June 1952.

45 Henry Nxumalo, 'Sugar Farms: Mr Drum Finds Out', *Drum* magazine, February 1953.

46 *Rand Daily Mail*, 'Koster Farmer Said He Told Son to Hit Native Convict', 23 September 1954.

47 Henry Nxumalo, 'I Worked at Snyman's Farm', *Drum* magazine, March 1955, 33.

48 Nxumalo, 'I Worked at Snyman's Farm', 35.

49 Nxumalo, 'I Worked at Snyman's Farm', 35.

50 Derrida, 'Archive Fever', 55.

51 Edith Rheinallt Jones, 'Farm Labour in the Transvaal'.

52 Joseph Lelyveld, 'One of the Least-Known Countries in the World', in *House of Bondage*, by Ernest Cole (New York: Random House, 1967), 13.

53 Karl Marx, *Capital*, vol. 1 (Knoxville, TN: Wordsworth Classics of World Literature, 2013), 541.

54 *Rand Daily Mail*, 'Victim's "Ghost" Made Man Confess to Murder', 12 August 1958.

Chapter 4: Violence: The white farmers' fears erupt

1   Lewis Nkosi, *Mating Birds* (Cape Town: Kwela Books, 2004), 84.

2   Cornelius Muller, 'Coercive Agrarian Work in South Africa, 1948–1960: "Farm Labour Scandal"?', MA thesis, University of Pretoria, 2011, 55–93.

3   Deborah Posel, 'Influx Control and Urban Labour Markets', in *Apartheid's Genesis: 1935–1962*, ed. Phil Bonner, Peter Delius and Deborah Posel (Johannesburg: Ravan Press, 1993), 413.

4   Posel, 'Influx Control and Urban Labour Markets', 413–414.

5   David Arnold, 'The Colonial Prison: Power, Knowledge and Penology in Nineteenth-Century India', *Subaltern Studies* 8 (1994): 146.

6   First, 'Exposure! The Farm Labour Scandal', 16.

7   First, 'Exposure! The Farm Labour Scandal', 16.

8   P.J. de Beer cited in Van Wyk and Ngakane, 'Pass Offenders and Farm Labour'.

9   Van Wyk and Ngakane, 'Pass Offenders and Farm Labour'.

10 Muller, 'Coercive Agrarian Work in South Africa,' 81.

11 First, 'Exposure! The Farm Labour Scandal', 16.

12 V.R. Verster (Commissioner of Prisons), 'Prisoners', Letter to South African Institute of Race Relations Research Officer, 16 February 1960, AD 1947/25.3, Historical Papers Research Archive.

13 *The Star*, 'Scramble for Labour is Root Cause', 13 March 1957.

14 M.L. Weston, Letter to South African Institute of Race Relations, 11 June 1959, AD 1947/25.1.3, Historical Papers Research Archive.

15 Horrel, Letter to M.L. Weston, 12 June 1959, AD 1947/25.1.3, Historical Papers Research Archive.

16 First, 'Exposure! The Farm Labour Scandal', 4.

17 Archie Mafeje, 'South Africa: The Dynamics of a Beleaguered State', *African Journal of Political Economy* 1, no. 1 (1986).

18 Higginson, *Collective Violence and the Agrarian Origins of South African Apartheid*, 20.

19 Murray, 'Factories in the Fields', 84.

20 Lacey, *Working for Boroko*, 19–24.

21 Lacey, *Working for Boroko*, 44.

22 Scott, 'Memorandum on Compound Labour Conditions'.

23 *Rand Daily Mail*, 'Readers' Points of Views: Apathy about Bethal. Is It Simply Force of Habit?', 21 July 1947.

24 Nxumalo, 'Bethal Today', 4.

25 First, 'Exposure! The Farm Labour Scandal', 20.

26 First, 'Exposure! The Farm Labour Scandal', 20.

27 First, 'Exposure! The Farm Labour Scandal', 20.

28 South African Institute of Race Relations, 'Memorandum for Committee of Inquiry into Farm Labour', 30 July 1959, AD 1947/25.5, Historical Papers Research Archive.

29 Scott, 'Memorandum on Compound Labour Conditions', 10.

30 William Edward Burghardt Du Bois, *The Souls of Black Folk* (New York: Oxford University Press, 2007), 29–32.

31 South African Institute of Race Relations, 'Memorandum for Committee of Inquiry into Farm Labour'.

32 Benjamin, *Reflections*.

33 Du Bois, *The Souls of Black Folk*, 120–121.

34 Ivan Evans, *Cultures of Violence: Lynching and Radical Killing in South Africa and the American South* (Manchester: Manchester University Press, 2009), 208.

35 L. Kraft, Letter to the South African Institute of Race Relations, 15 July 1957, AD 1947/25.1.3, General Correspondence from 1954–1962, Historical Papers Research Archive.

36 Van Wyk and Ngakane, 'Pass Offenders and Farm Labour'.

37 Higginson, *Collective Violence and the Agrarian Origins of South African Apartheid*, 21.

38 Higginson, *Collective Violence and the Agrarian Origins of South African Apartheid*, 90.

39 Anthony Marx, *Making Race and Nation: A Comparison of the United States, South Africa, and Brazil* (Cambridge: Cambridge University Press, 1998), 82.

40 Marx, *Making Race and Nation*, 270.

41 Francis Wilson, 'Farm, 1866–1966', in *The Oxford History of South Africa*, vol. 2, ed. Monica Wilson and Leonard Thompson (Oxford: Clarendon Press, 1971), 104.

42 Jean-Paul Sartre, Preface to *The Wretched of the Earth*, by Frantz Fanon (London: Penguin, 1967), 13–14.

43 Duncan, *South Africa's Rule of Violence*, 13.

44 Duncan, *South Africa's Rule of Violence*, 96.

45 See Worden, *The Making of Modern South Africa*; Tom Lodge, 'Political Mobilisation During the 1950s: An East London Case Study', in *The Politics of Race, Class and Nationalism in Twentieth-Century South Africa*, ed. Shula Marks and Stanley Trapido (London: Longman, 1987); Peter Delius, *A Lion amongst the Cattle: Reconstruction and Resistance in the Northern Transvaal* (Johannesburg: Ravan Press, 1996); Karis and Gerhart, *Challenge and Violence 1953–1964*.

Chapter 5: These eyes are looking for a home

1 Oscar Wilde, *The Picture of Dorian Gray* (London: Penguin Classics, 2000), 61.

2 Plaatje, *Native Life in South Africa*, 104.

3 Julien Benda, *The Treason of the Intellectuals* (New Brunswick and London: Transaction Publishers, 2014), 36–37.

4 No Sizwe (Neville Alexander), *One Azania, One Nation: The National Question in South Africa* (London: Zed Press, 1979), 11.

5 Frantz Fanon, *Black Skin, White Masks* (London: Pluto Press, 1986), 83.

6 Ms Mkhwanazi, interview.

7 Ms Mkhwanazi, interview.

8 Plaatje, *Native Life in South Africa*, 65.

9 V.S. Welsford, Letters dated 27 July 1953; 13 August 1953; 15 August 1953; 4 December 1953; 8 December 1953; AD 1947/25.1.3, General Correspondence from 1954–1962, Historical Papers Research Archive.

10 Frederick van Wyk, Letters to Mr V.S. Welsford, 15 December 1953; 11 March 1954; AD 1947/25.1.3, General Correspondence from 1954–1962, Historical Papers Research Archive.

11 Du Toit, 'Paternalism and Modernity on South African Wine and Fruit Farms', 56.

12 Mr Nsibande, interview.

13 Ms Mkhwanazi, interview.

14 South African Agricultural Union (n.d.), 'Native Policy for Agriculture', AD 1947/25.5, Historical Papers Research Archive.

15 See John David Rheinallt Jones (n.d.), 'Native Farm Labour Suggestion for Improving Conditions', AD 1947/25.5 (2.5.5.10), Historical Papers Research Archive.

16 South African Agricultural Union, 'Native Policy for Agriculture'.

17 South African Agricultural Union, 'Native Policy for Agriculture'.

18 South African Agricultural Union, 'Native Policy for Agriculture'.

19 South African Institute of Race Relations, 'Memorandum for Committee of Inquiry into Farm Labour'.

20 Margaret Robert, 'Labour in the Farm Economy', 1958, AD 1947/25.5, Historical Papers Research Archive.

21 Edith Rheinallt Jones, 'Farm Labour in the Transvaal'.

22 Duncan, *South Africa's Rule of Violence*, 127.

23 Ms Mkhwanazi, interview.

24 Mr Ngubeza Mahlangu, interview.

25 Jackie Grobler, *A Decisive Clash? A Short History of Black Protest Politics in South Africa: 1875–1976* (Pretoria: Acacia Books, 1988), 114.

26 Mr with Mrs Nkosi, interviewed by Tshepo Moloi, eMzinoni, Bethal, 21 August 2008.

27 See Robert Edgar and Luyanda ka Msumza (eds.), *Africa's Cause Must Triumph: The Collected Writings of A.P. Mda* (Cape Town: HSRC Press, 2018), 45–51.

28 Karis and Gerhart, *Challenge and Violence 1953–1964*, 292.

29 *Rand Daily Mail*, 'Inquest Told of Farm Labourer's Beating'.

30 See Nair, 'Through the Eyes of the Workers'; Karis and Gerhart, *Challenge and Violence 1953–1964*; Muller, 'Coercive Agrarian Work in South Africa'.

31 Grobler, *A Decisive Clash?*, 114.

32 Nair, 'Through the Eyes of the Workers', 170.

33 *The Star*, 'Farmers Bring Natives Back by Lorry Load', 8 June 1959.

34 *Rand Daily Mail*, 'Boycott Hits Potato Sales', 17 June 1959.

35 Tom Lodge, *Black Politics in South Africa Since 1945* (Johannesburg: Ravan Press, 1983), 91–113.

36 Jeremy Baskin, *Striking Back: A History of COSATU* (New York: Verso, 1991), 14.

37 Ian Edwards, 'Cato Manor, June 1959: Men, Women, Crowds, Violence, Politics and History', in *The People's City: African Life in Twentieth-Century Durban*, ed. Paul Maylam and Ian Edwards (Pietermaritzburg: University of Natal Press, 1996).

38 See Cedric Robinson, *Black Marxism: The Making of the Black Radical Tradition* (Chapel Hill: University of North Carolina Press, 2000), 241–286; Penny M. von Eschen, *Race Against Empire: Black Americans and Anticolonialism, 1937–57* (Ithaca, NY, and London: Cornell University Press, 1997), 2.

39 Roger Southall, *Whites and Democracy in South Africa* (Stellenbosch: African Sun Media, 2022), 1.

40 Ralph Ellison cited in Penny M. von Eschen, *Race Against Empire*, 6.

41 Eric R. Wolf, *Peasant Wars of the Twentieth Century* (New York: Harper & Row, 1968); Cedric Robinson, *Black Marxism*, 168.

42 Govan Mbeki, *South Africa: The Peasants' Revolt* (London: International Defence and Aid Fund for Southern Africa, 1984), 111.

43 Ms Mkhwanazi, interview.

44 Mr Ngubeza Mahlangu, interview.

Chapter 6: Bethal today

1   Styles Ledwaba and Jürgen Schadeberg, 'Bethal Today', in *Voices from the Land*, ed. Jürgen Schadeberg (Pretoria: Protea Book House, 2005).

2   Schadeberg, *The Way I See It*, 170.

3   Ledwaba and Schadeberg, 'Bethal Today'.

4   Scott, 'Memorandum on Compound Labour Conditions'.

5   This is the farm Schadeberg went to in order to fetch Henry Nxumalo (see Schadeberg, *The Way I See It*, 170).

6   First, 'Exposure! The Farm Labour Scandal', 3.

7   Mr Mathebe, interviewed by uMbuso weNkosi, Blesbokspruit farm, Bethal, 19 September 2021.

8   Mr Soko, interview.

9   Oliver Sacks, *The River of Consciousness* (New York: Alfred A. Knopf, 2017).

10 Mr Sithole [not his real name], interviewed by uMbuso weNkosi, Legdaar farm, Bethal, 17 September 2001.

11 Mr Sithole, interview.

12 Mr Mazibuko, interviewed by uMbuso weNkosi, Legdaar farm, Bethal, 17 September 2021.

13 A. Hoedemaker, Letters.

14 Lelyveld, 'One of the Least-Known Countries in the World', 10.

15 Mr Mathebe, interview.

16 Mr Mathebe, interview.

17 Mr Mathebe, interview.

18 Mr Mahlangu, interviewed by uMbuso weNkosi, Blesbokspruit farm, Bethal, 19 September 2021.

19 Mbuso Nkosi, 'Doing Research Otherwise', 179.

20 Mr Mazibuko, interview.

21 Mr Mazibuko, interview.

22 Mr Mavuso [not his real name], interviewed by uMbuso weNkosi, Legdaar farm, Bethal, 17 September 2021.

23 Mr Mavuso, interview.

24 Mr Mazibuko, interview.

25 Mr Mazibuko, interview.

26 Mr Groebler, interview.

27 South African Government, Extension of Security of Tenure Act 62 of 1997, https://www.gov.za/documents/extension-security-tenure-act, accessed 8 March 2023.

28 Mr Mazibuko, interview.

29 This point is well made by Marc Wegerif, Bev Russell and Irma Grundling, 'Still Searching for Security: The Reality of Farm Dweller Evictions in South Africa', Nkuzi Development Association, Johannesburg, 2005. The authors were able to show how labour tenants were removed from the land despite the existence of laws that protect them in democratic South Africa.

30 Mr Moses Magwaza [not his real name], interviewed by uMbuso weNkosi, Schurvekop farm, Bethal, 18 September 2021.

Chapter 7: Our eschatological future

1 Fyodor Dostoevsky, 'The House of the Dead' and 'Poor Folk' (New York: Barnes & Noble Classics, 2004), 202.

2 Georg Wilhelm Friedrich Hegel, The Phenomenology of Spirit (London: Oxford University Press, 1977), 114.

3 Plaatje, Native Life in South Africa, 55–56.

4 A point already made by Jonny Steinberg in his seminal book Midlands (Johannesburg and Cape Town: Jonathan Ball, 2002).

5 To Levinas, '[t]he alterity of the other is not a particular case, a species of alterity, but its original exception. It is not because the other is new, an unheard of quiddity, that he signifies transcendence, or, more exactly, signifies, purely and simply; it is because newness comes from the other that there is in newness transcendence and signification. It is through the other that newness signifies in being the otherwise than being. Without the proximity of the other in his face everything is absorbed, sunken into, walled in being, goes to the same side, forms a whole, absorbing the very subject to which it is disclosed.' Levinas, Otherwise than Being or Beyond Essence, 182.

6   Abdul R. JanMohamed refers to this as death-bound-subjectivity, where the
      violence by the white society aims to produce a subjectivity amongst Black
      people whose subjecthood 'is formed, from infancy on, by the imminent and
      ubiquitous threat of death'. See Abdul R. JanMohamed, *The Death-Bound-
      Subject: Richard Wright's Archaeology of Death* (Durham, NC: Duke University
      Press, 2005).

Bibliography

Africa Check. 'Report of the Committee of Inquiry into Farm Attacks', 31 July 2003. https://africacheck.org/sites/default/files/Final-Report-Committee-of-Inquiry-Farm-Attacks-July-2003.pdf. Accessed 2 December 2015.

Ainslie, Rosalynde. *Masters and Serfs: Farm Labour in South Africa.* London: International Defence and Aid Fund for Southern Africa, 1977.

Arnold, David. 'The Colonial Prison: Power, Knowledge and Penology in Nineteenth-Century India'. *Subaltern Studies* 8 (1994): 146.

Ashforth, Adam. 'On the Native Question: A Reading of the Grand Tradition of Commissions of Inquiry into the "Native Question" in Twentieth-Century South Africa'. PhD thesis, Oxford University, 1987.

Baard, Frances. *My Spirit Is Not Banned.* Harare: Zimbabwe Publishing House, 1986. https://www.sahistory.org.za/archive/dont-eat-potatoes. Accessed 1 December 2021.

Baskin, Jeremy. *Striking Back: A History of COSATU.* New York: Verso, 1991.

Benda, Julien. *The Treason of the Intellectuals.* New Brunswick and London: Transaction Publishers, 2014.

Benjamin, Walter. *Reflections: Essays, Aphorisms, Autobiographical Writing.* New York: Schocken Books, 1986.

Bothma, G.P., W.A. de Klerk, C.B. Ehlers and J.H. van Niekerk. 'Bethal 1880–1980 – Eeufees Gedenkalbum'. Bethal: Bethal Stadsraad, 1980.

Bradford, Helen. *A Taste of Freedom: The ICU in Rural South Africa, 1924–1930.* Johannesburg: Ravan Press, 1988.

De Kiewiet, Cornelius William. *A History of South Africa: Social and Economic.* London: Oxford University Press, 1941.

Delius, Peter. *A Lion amongst the Cattle: Reconstruction and Resistance in the Northern Transvaal.* Johannesburg: Ravan Press, 1996.

Derrida, Jacques. 'Archive Fever: A Freudian Impression'. *Diacritics* 25, no. 2 (Summer 1995): 9–63.

Derrida, Jacques. *The Gift of Death.* Chicago: University of Chicago Press, 1995.

157

Dostoevsky, Fyodor. 'The House of the Dead' and 'Poor Folk'. New York: Barnes & Noble Classics, 2004.

Du Bois, William Edward Burghardt. *Black Reconstruction in America 1860–1880: An Essay Toward a History of the Part which Black Folk Played in the Attempt to Reconstruct Democracy in America*. Cleveland and New York: World Publishing Company, 1935.

Du Bois, William Edward Burghardt. *The Souls of Black Folk*. New York: Oxford University Press, 2007.

Duncan, Patrick. *South Africa's Rule of Violence*. London: Methuen, 1964.

Durkheim, Emile. *The Division of Labour in Society*. London: Macmillan Press, 1984.

Du Toit, Andries. 'Paternalism and Modernity on South African Wine and Fruit Farms: An Analysis of Paternalist Constructions of Community and Authority in the Discourse of Coloured Farm Workers in the Stellenbosch Region'. PhD thesis, University of Essex, 1996.

Edgar, Robert and Luyanda ka Msumza, eds. *Africa's Cause Must Triumph: The Collected Writings of A.P. Mda*. Cape Town: HSRC Press, 2018.

Edwards, Ian. 'Cato Manor, June 1959: Men, Women, Crowds, Violence, Politics and History'. In *The People's City: African Life in Twentieth-Century Durban*, edited by Paul Maylam and Ian Edwards, 102–142. Pietermaritzburg: University of Natal Press, 1996.

Ellison, Ralph. *Invisible Man*. London: Penguin Classics, 1952.

Evans, Ivan. *Cultures of Violence: Lynching and Radical Killing in South Africa and the American South*. Manchester: Manchester University Press, 2009.

Fairbrother, Bevis. 'My Take: Politicians Now CSI Experts?' *South Coast Herald*, 28 March 2015. https://southcoastherald.co.za/81596/my-take-politicians-now-csi-experts/. Accessed 4 April 2016.

Fanon, Frantz. *Black Skin, White Masks*. London: Pluto Press, 1986.

First, Ruth. 'Bethal Case-Book'. *Africa South* 2, no. 3 (1958): 14–25.

First, Ruth. 'Exposure! The Farm Labour Scandal'. *New Age* pamphlet, 1959.

Foucault, Michel. *The History of Sexuality*. Vol. 1, *An Introduction*. New York: Pantheon Books, 1978.

Grobler, Jackie. *A Decisive Clash? A Short History of Black Protest Politics in South Africa: 1875–1976*. Pretoria: Acacia Books, 1988.

Hegel, Georg Wilhelm Friedrich. *The Phenomenology of Spirit*. London: Oxford University Press, 1977.

Higginson, John. *Collective Violence and the Agrarian Origins of South African Apartheid*. New York: Cambridge University Press, 2015.

JanMohamed, Abdul R. *The Death-Bound-Subject: Richard Wright's Archaeology of Death*. Durham, NC: Duke University Press, 2005.

Karis, Thomas and Gail M. Gerhart. *Challenge and Violence 1953–1964.* Vol. 3 of *From Protest to Challenge: A Documentary History of African Politics in South Africa 1882–1964,* edited by Thomas G. Karis and Gail M. Gerhart. Stanford, CA: Hoover Institution Press, 1977.

Khoza, Amanda. 'Sangoma Tells How She Located KZN Graves'. *The Witness,* 24 March 2015. https://www.news24.com/SouthAfrica/News/Sangoma-tells-how-she-located-KZN-graves-20150324. Accessed 4 April 2016.

Lacey, Marian. *Working for Boroko: The Origins of a Coercive Labour System in South Africa.* Johannesburg: Ravan Press, 1981.

Ledwaba, Styles and Jürgen Schadeberg. 'Bethal Today'. In *Voices from the Land,* edited by Jürgen Schadeberg. Pretoria: Protea Book House, 2005.

Lelyveld, Joseph. 'One of the Least-Known Countries in the World'. In *House of Bondage,* by Ernest Cole, 7–19. New York: Random House, 1967.

Levinas, Emmanuel. *Alterity and Transcendence.* London: Athlone Press, 1999.

Levinas, Emmanuel. *Otherwise than Being or Beyond Essence.* Translated by Alphonso Lingis. The Hague: Nijhoff Publishers, 1974.

Levinas, Emmanuel. *Totality and Infinity: An Essay on Exteriority.* The Hague: Nijhoff Publishers, 1969.

Lodge, Tom. *Black Politics in South Africa Since 1945.* Johannesburg: Ravan Press, 1983.

Lodge, Tom. 'Political Mobilisation During the 1950s: An East London Case Study'. In *The Politics of Race, Class and Nationalism in Twentieth-Century South Africa,* edited by Shula Marks and Stanley Trapido, 310–315. London: Longman, 1987.

Mafeje, Archie. 'South Africa: The Dynamics of a Beleaguered State'. *African Journal of Political Economy* 1, no. 1 (1986): 95–119.

Manda, Sihle. 'Tortured Souls of Dududu'. *IOL,* 24 March 2015. http://www.iol.co.za/news/south-africa/kwazulu-natal/tortured-souls-of-dududu-1836293. Accessed 4 April 2016.

Marx, Anthony. *Making Race and Nation: A Comparison of the United States, South Africa, and Brazil.* Cambridge: Cambridge University Press, 1998.

Marx, Karl. *Capital,* vol. 1. Knoxville, TN: Wordsworth Classics of World Literature, 2013.

Mbeki, Govan. *South Africa: The Peasants' Revolt.* London: International Defence and Aid Fund for Southern Africa, 1984.

Mignolo, Walter D. 'Epistemic Disobedience, Independent Thought and De-Colonial Freedom'. *Theory, Culture & Society* 26, no. 7–8 (2009): 159–181.

Mitchell, Timothy. *Colonising Egypt.* Berkeley: University of California Press, 1991.

Mthethwa, Bongani, Mathew Savides and Taschica Pillay. 'Unearthing the Secrets of KwaZulu-Natal's Farm of Horrors'. *TimesLive,* 27 March 2015. https://www.

timeslive.co.za/news/south-africa/2015-03-27-unearthing-the-secrets-of-kwazulu-natals-farm-of-horrors/. Accessed 4 April 2016.

Muller, Cornelius. 'Coercive Agrarian Work in South Africa, 1948–1960: "Farm Labour Scandal"?' MA thesis, University of Pretoria, 2011.

Murray, Martin. 'Factories in the Fields: Capitalist Farming in the Bethal District, 1910–1950'. In *White Farms, Black Labor: The State and Agrarian Change in Southern Africa*, edited by Alan Jeeves and Jonathan Crush. Portsmouth: Heinemann, 1997.

Nair, Billy. 'Through the Eyes of the Workers'. In *Reflections in Prison: Voices from the South African Liberation Struggle*, edited by Mac Maharaj. Amherst and Boston: University of Massachusetts Press, 2001.

Nkosi, Lewis. *Mating Birds*. Cape Town: Kwela Books, 2004.

Nkosi, Mandla. 'Why Potato Boycott was Called Off'. *New Age*, 10 September 1959.

Nkosi, Mbuso. 'Doing Research Otherwise: Critical Essays on "the Land Question", Farmworkers and Resistance in South Africa'. PhD dissertation, University of the Witwatersrand, 2018.

No Sizwe (Neville Alexander). *One Azania, One Nation: The National Question in South Africa*. London: Zed Press, 1979.

Pillay, Kamcilla and Nosipho Mngoma. 'Mass Graves Found on KZN Farm'. *IOL*, 16 March 2015. https://www.iol.co.za/news/crime-courts/mass-graves-found-on-kzn-farm-1832544. Accessed 4 April 2016.

Plaatje, Solomon. *Native Life in South Africa, Before and Since the European War and the Boer Rebellion*. Urbana, IL: Project Gutenberg, 1998.

Posel, Deborah. 'Influx Control and Urban Labour Markets'. In *Apartheid's Genesis: 1935–1962*, edited by Phil Bonner, Peter Delius and Deborah Posel. Johannesburg: Ravan Press, 1993.

Posel, Deborah. *The Making of Apartheid 1948–1961: Conflict and Compromise*. Oxford: Clarendon Press, 1991.

Redcliffe, Salaman. *The History and Social Influence of the Potato*. Cambridge: Cambridge University Press, 1949.

Rich, Paul. 'Segregation and the Cape Liberal Tradition'. Collected Seminar Papers. Institute of Commonwealth Studies 26 (1981): 31–41.

Robinson, Cedric. *Black Marxism: The Making of the Black Radical Tradition*. Chapel Hill: University of North Carolina Press, 2000.

Rousseau, Nicky. 'The Farm, the River and the Picnic Spot: Topographies of Terror'. *African Studies* 68, no. 3 (2009): 351–369.

Sacks, Oliver. *The River of Consciousness*. New York: Alfred A. Knopf, 2017.

Sampson, Anthony. *Drum: A Venture into the New Africa*. London: Collins, 1956.

Sartre, Jean-Paul. Preface to *The Wretched of the Earth*, by Frantz Fanon. London: Penguin Books, 1967.

Schadeberg, Jürgen. *The Way I See It: A Memoir*. Johannesburg: Picador Africa, 2017.

Segal, Lauren. *A Brutal Harvest: The Roots and Legitimation of Violence on Farms in South Africa*. Johannesburg: Black Sash, 1991.

Smith, Linda T. *Decolonizing Methodologies: Research and Indigenous Peoples*. London: Zed Books, 1999.

Southall, Roger. *Whites and Democracy in South Africa*. Stellenbosch: African Sun Media, 2022.

Spillers, Hortense J. 'Mama's Baby, Papa's Maybe: An American Grammar Book'. In 'Culture and Countermemory: The "American" Connection', special issue, *Diacritics* 17, no. 2 (Summer 1987): 64–81.

Stanley, Liz. *Mourning Becomes ... Post/memory, Commemoration and the Concentration Camps of the South African War*. Johannesburg: Wits University Press, 2008.

Steinberg, Jonny. *Midlands*. Johannesburg and Cape Town: Jonathan Ball, 2002.

Taylor, Frederick Winslow. *The Principles of Scientific Management*. New York: Harper & Brothers, 1947.

Thompson, Leonard Monteath. *The Unification of South Africa, 1902–1910*. Oxford: Clarendon Press, 1960.

Van Onselen, Charles. 'The Social and Economic Underpinning of Paternalism and Violence on the Maize Farms of the South-Western Transvaal, 1900–1950'. *Journal of Historical Sociology* 5, no. 2 (June 1992): 129–131.

Von Eschen, Penny M. *Race Against Empire: Black Americans and Anticolonialism, 1937–57*. Ithaca, NY, and London: Cornell University Press, 1997.

Walker, Cheryl and Ben Cousins. 'Land Divided, Land Restored: Introduction'. In *Land Divided Land Restored: Land Reform in South Africa for the 21st Century*, edited by Ben Cousins and Cheryl Walker. Johannesburg: Jacana Media, 2015.

Wegerif, Marc, Bev Russell and Irma Grundling. 'Still Searching for Security: The Reality of Farm Dweller Evictions in South Africa'. Nkuzi Development Association, Johannesburg, 2005.

Wilde, Oscar. *The Picture of Dorian Grey*. London: Penguin Classics, 2000.

Wilson, Francis. 'Farm, 1866–1966'. In *The Oxford History of South Africa*, vol. 2, edited by Monica Wilson and Leonard Thompson. Oxford: Clarendon Press, 1971.

Wolf, Eric R. *Peasant Wars of the Twentieth Century*. New York: Harper & Row, 1968.

Worden, Nigel. *The Making of Modern South Africa: Conquest, Apartheid, Democracy*. Chichester: Wiley-Blackwell, 2012.

Yates, Anne and Lewis Chester. *The Troublemaker: Michael Scott and His Lonely Struggle Against Injustice*. London: Aurum Press, 2006.

HISTORICAL PAPERS RESEARCH ARCHIVE
University of the Witwatersrand, Johannesburg

Assistant Director of Native Agriculture in Flagstaff. Re: Training of Natives in Agricultural Colleges. Letter to Quintin Whyte, 19 July 1948. AD 1947/25.1.1. General Correspondence from 1947–1950.

Hansard, no. 20-16/6/59, col. 8202-8203. AD 1947/25.4.

Hoedemaker, A. Letters to Frederick van Wyk (acting director of South African Institute of Race Relations), 24 March 1952; 2 April 1952. AD 1947/25.1.2. Farm Labour General Correspondence 1951–1953.

Horrel. Letter to M.L. Weston, 12 June 1959. AD 1947/25.1.3.

Kraft, L. Letter to the South African Institute of Race Relations, 15 July 1957. AD 1947/25.1.3. General Correspondence from 1954–1962.

Moloke, Timothy. Letter to the South African Institute of Race Relations, 23 May 1953. AD 1947/25.1.2. Farm Labour General Correspondence 1951–1953.

National Organiser of the Penal Reform League of South Africa. Letter addressed to the Director of Prisons in Cape Town, 12 May 1952. AD 1947/25.3.

Ngakane, William Barney. Letter to Henri-Philippe Junod, 15 March 1954. AD 1947/25.3.

Ngakane, William Barney. 'Report of Inquiry into the Working Conditions of Prison Farm Labourers'. South African Institute of Race Relations. AD 1947/25.3.

Rheinallt Jones, Edith. 'Farm Labour in the Transvaal'. *Race Relations Journal* 12, no. 1, 1945. AD 1947/25.5.

Rheinallt Jones, John David (n.d.). 'Native Farm Labour Suggestion for Improving Conditions'. AD 1947/25.5 (2.5.5.10).

Robert, Margaret. 'Labour in the Farm Economy', 1958. AD 1947/25.5.

Scott, Michael. 'Memorandum on Compound Labour Conditions in Agriculture, Bethal District', 1947. AB684f.

South African Agricultural Union (n.d.). 'Native Policy for Agriculture'. AD 1947/25.5.

South African Institute of Race Relations. 'Memorandum for Committee of Inquiry into Farm Labour', 30 July 1959. AD 1947/25.5.

Transvaal Government Gazette, no. 213, Tuesday, 12 October 1880.

Van Wyk, Frederick J. Letters to Mrs A. Hoedemaker, 3 March 1952; 19 May 1952. AD 1947/25.1.2. Farm Labour General Correspondence 1951–1953.

Van Wyk, Frederick. Letters to Mr V.S. Welsford, 15 December 1953; 11 March 1954. AD 1947/25.1.3. General Correspondence from 1954–1962.

Van Wyk, Frederick and William Barney Ngakane. 'Pass Offenders and Farm Labour'. 21 September 1949. AD 1947/25.2.

Verster, V.R. (Commissioner of Prisons). 'Prisoners'. Letter to South African Institute of Race Relations Research Officer, 16 February 1960. AD 1947/25.3.

Welsford, V.S. Letters dated 27 July 1953; 13 August 1953; 15 August 1953; 4 December 1953; 8 December 1953. AD 1947 25.1.3. General Correspondence from 1954–1962.

Weston, M.L. Letter to South African Institute of Race Relations, 11 June 1959. AD 1947/25.1.3.

NEWSPAPER AND MAGAZINE ARTICLES

Drum magazine. Nxumalo, Henry. 'Bethal Today: *Drum*'s Fearless Exposure of Human Exploitation', April 1952.

Drum magazine. Nxumalo, Henry. 'I Worked at Snyman's Farm', March 1955.

Drum magazine. Nxumalo, Henry. 'Mr Drum Looks at the Tot System', June 1952.

Drum magazine. Nxumalo, Henry. 'Sugar Farms: Mr Drum Finds Out', February 1953.

Rand Daily Mail. 'Bethal an Ideal Holiday Resort and Residential Centre', 25 May 1936.

Rand Daily Mail. 'Bethal Farmers Vindicated, Says Lawrence: Allegations of Widespread Abuses Unfounded', 21 July 1947.

Rand Daily Mail. 'Boycott Hits Potato Sales', 17 June 1959.

Rand Daily Mail. 'Farmer Fined for Beating Convicts', 28 May 1959.

Rand Daily Mail. 'Inquest Told of Farm Labourer's Beating', 9 July 1959.

Rand Daily Mail. 'Koster Farmer Said He Told Son to Hit Native Convict', 23 September 1954.

Rand Daily Mail. 'Readers' Points of Views: Apathy about Bethal. Is It Simply Force of Habit?', 21 July 1947.

Rand Daily Mail. 'Three Farm Foremen Fined', 21 July 1947.

Rand Daily Mail. 'Victim's "Ghost" Made Man Confess to Murder', 12 August 1958.

The Star. 'Farmers Bring Natives Back by Lorry Load', 8 June 1959.

The Star. 'Scramble for Labour is Root Cause', 13 March 1957.

Sunday Times. 'Farm Labour: Another Body Exhumed', 21 June 1959.

INTERVIEWS

Mr Groebler, interviewed by uMbuso weNkosi and Xender Ehlers, Bethal, 15 October 2021.

Mr Moses Magwaza [not his real name], interviewed by uMbuso weNkosi, Schurvekop farm, Bethal, 18 September 2021.

Mr Mahlangu, interviewed by uMbuso weNkosi, Blesbokspruit farm, Bethal, 19 September 2021.

Mr Ngubeza Mahlangu, interviewed by Tshepo Moloi, eMzinoni, Bethal, 4 August 2008.

Mr Mathebe, interviewed by uMbuso weNkosi, Blesbokspruit farm, Bethal, 19 September 2021.

Mr Mavuso [not his real name], interviewed by uMbuso weNkosi, Legdaar farm, Bethal, 17 September 2021.

Mr Mazibuko, interviewed by uMbuso weNkosi, Legdaar farm, Bethal, 17 September 2021.

Ms Elizabeth Mkhwanazi, interviewed by Tshepo Moloi, eMzinoni, Bethal, 20 August 2008.

Mr with Mrs Nkosi, interviewed by Tshepo Moloi, eMzinoni, Bethal, 21 August 2008.

Mr Mavumeni John Nsibande, interviewed by Tshepo Moloi, eMzinoni, Bethal, 21 August 2008.

Mr Sithole [not his real name], interviewed by uMbuso weNkosi, Legdaar farm, Bethal, 17 September 2021.

Mr Soko, interviewed by uMbuso weNkosi, eMzinoni, Bethal, 26 January 2020.

Index

Page numbers in *italics* indicate figures.

A

Ackerman, Matthys Stufnus 69
activists *16*, 17, 49
Adam, Usuman 91
Africanism 110
African National Congress (ANC) 10–12,
    15, 37, 90, 109
African National Congress Women's
    League (ANCWL) 15
African Residential Association 62–63
Afrikaners 17–18, 52, 85–87, 93–94
agriculture 4, 33–34, 45, 52–54, 57–58, 79,
    82–89, 116
alcohol 70
Alexander, Neville (No Sizwe) 100
alterity 15, 20, 118–119
ama joints *see* contract workers
America *see* United States of America
ANC *see* African National Congress
ancestors 1, 17–20, 74–75, 82, 120–121,
    125–126, 129–130, 132
ANCWL *see* African National Congress
    Women's League
Anglo-Boer War 17–18, 52, *53*, 92–94
Anthony, Paul 90
anxiety of white society 13–14, 17, 23, 26,
    50, 52, 75–78, 89–99, 112, 126–128,
    131–136
apartheid 12, 17–18, 38–39, 96, 99, 112,
    126–127, 134–136

archaeology 39–40, 119, 133
assault *see* violence

B

Baard, Frances 15
baas boys *see* boss-boys
bags *see* potato sacks
Banda, Samson 91
Bantu Education Act 113
belonging 19, 25, 28–30, 32, 35, 37, 50,
    121–129
    see also home
Benda, Julien 99
Bethal
    children *64*, *67*
    contract workers 58–63
    division of labour 63–66
    history of 51–54, *53*
    killings 38, 40–43
    potato boycott 6, 11–12
    research on 6, 7–10, 16
    visits to 28–29, 115–121, *117*, 138–139
    working conditions on farms 1–5, *2–3*,
        14, 35, 45–49, 54–58, *56*, *64*, 66–76,
        67, 85–88, 101, 132, 137
'Bethal Case-Book' (First) 54–55
'Bethal Today: *Drum*'s Fearless Exposure of
    Human Exploitation' (Nxumalo) 13
Bibles 55, 57
bitterness 43, 122–123

Black, defining being 27, 97–102
Black Consciousness movement 100, 113
'black danger' see 'swart gevaar'
Black Monday protest 135–136
Blesbokspruit farm 51, 117–118, 123–124, 129
boss-boys 55, 56, 62, 65–66, 67, 70–71, 116
Botha, S.P. 91
boycott see potato boycott
Brenkman, Balthasar Johannes 116–117
British East India Company 79
British Empire 54, 79
brutality see violence

C
Callinicos, Luli 6
capitalism 75–76, 85–87, 89
'captive body' 8
Carlson, Joel 90–91
cattle 19, 32–33, 124
challenge see resistance
children
    education 108
    as farmworkers 55, 63, 64, 67, 86, 103–105
    leaving farms 123, 129–130, 137
civil rights movement 112
clothes made from potato sacks 13, 14
Collective Violence and the Agrarian Origins of South African Apartheid, 1900–1948 (Higginson) 93–94
colonialism 18–20, 97, 125
Communist Party of South Africa 113
compounds 52–53, 57, 60, 66, 118
Congress Alliance 111
conscience, haunted 73, 76, 78
consent of prisoners 80–82, 90
contestation see resistance
contract workers 52, 55, 58–64, 70, 120
corruption 24, 81–82
criminality 32, 37, 45–46, 75, 78–80, 84, 91–95
Cultures of Violence (Evans) 92

D
dead bodies 11, 36–37, 50, 73, 102–103
    see also killings

death 8, 34–35, 102–103, 125, 138
    see also killings
De Beer, P.J. 12, 24, 34–35, 40–43, 49, 81–82, 92
debt to farmers 64, 70
De Clercq, Hendrick 103
decolonisation 112
Decolonizing Methodologies (Smith) 9
Department of Arts and Culture 36
Department of Justice 65
Department of Native Affairs 40, 58
Department of Prisons 1–5, 2–3
Derrida, Jacques 8, 73
desertion 4, 46–48, 61–62, 71, 84
detribalised 79
De Wet Nel, M.D.C. 66
discipline see punishment
dispossession see land dispossession
docility 10, 75–76, 95, 105
'dop system' 70
Dostoevsky, Fyodor 131
Drum 13, 55, 59, 61–62, 70, 87, 115–118
Dube, Nelson 91
Dube, Victor 76
Du Bois, W.E.B. 8, 90, 92
Duncan, Patrick 95–96
Du Plooij, Cornelius Michiel 51
Du Toit, Andries 21

E
economic view of land question 33–34
education 27, 98–99, 104–109
Ehlers, Xender 28, 116
Ellison, Ralph 8, 112
emazambaneni (land of potatoes) 4
eMsinga, KwaZulu-Natal 36
eMzinoni township 119–120
England see British Empire
eschatological future 23, 130, 133, 136–137
eschatological gaze 15, 20, 24–25, 33, 49, 115, 118–121, 125
eschatological terror 82
ethical relationship with land 18–19, 21
ethics 8–9, 49, 97–98, 118–119
Evans, Ivan 92
eviction 31, 128–129

expropriation without compensation 21, 34, 125, 137–138
Extension of Security of Tenure Act 121, 128–129
eyes
  looking at history 23–25, 31–35, 40–43, 49–50, 97–98, 133
  as prejudiced 33–34, 136–137
  theorising from 49–50
'eyes', of potatoes 14–15
ezintandaneni (place of orphans) 37

F
Fanon, Frantz 95
farmers
  anxiety of 13–14, 17, 23, 62–63, 99, 134–135
  expropriation without compensation 21
  farmworkers and 13, 23, 26–27, 37, 40–49, 57–58, 64–65, 77–78, 95–96, 123–126
  as law 17, 58–62, 92–95, 121, 129, 135
  names for 72–73, 119
  paternalism 21–22, 66–76, 136
  state and 35, 45–49, 65, 80–85
  unions 83
farming see agriculture
farm prisons 14, 65–66, 75, 82–84, 107
farms
  apartheid and 18
  as invisible space 92
  visits to 28–29, 116–118, *117*
Farmworkers' Association 110
fear see anxiety of white society; terror
Feldt, B. 90
First, Ruth 12, 54–55, 63–64, 80, 88–89, 118
flag, of apartheid state 135–136
Fordsburg, Johannesburg 34–35, 40–42
foremen 65–66
forensic eye 34, 39–40
freedom 36, 38–40, 138
Freedom Charter 111
frozen in time 39–40
full-time workers 63
future
  eschatological 23, 130, 133, 136–137

land dispossession and 35, 135, 138
futurity of violence 9–10, 73–76, 87–88, 95–96, 108–109, 125–126, 131–132, 136

G
General Circular No. 23 of 1954 82
Genesis 28:16–17 51
genocide 21, 23, 135
Ghana 112
ghosts see spirits
Glenroy farm 34, 36–40
Gogo Mshanelo see Nkomo, Gogo Bongekile Nonhlanhla 'Mshanelo'
gold mining see mining
graves 31–32, 35–39, 50, 120–122, 125–126, 130
Group Areas Act 112
guardianship 106–107
  see also paternalism

H
happiness 42–43, 122–123
Harmonie farm 70–73
hell 54
Hertzog, J.B.M. 86
heuristic model 14, 102, 133
Higginson, John 93–94
Hirschowitz, Mr 90
Historical Papers Research Archive 1, 20–21
historical present 16, 31–32, 115–116, 118–121, 132, 137–138
Hoedemaker, A. 43–45, 122–123
home 51–63, 99, 113–114, 116–119, 121–126, 133–139
  see also belonging
hope 1, 32–33
Hudson, George 51

I
identity 27, 97–102
Illovo Sugar 36
immigrants 52, 54, 61, 63–64, 74, 86, 120
Immorality Act 112
industrialisation 85

influx control 78–79
iqunga 73, 131–132
Ireland 25

J
Julius Caesar (Shakespeare) 6–7
Junod, Henri-Philippe 4, 5, 69–70
justice 8, 73, 76

K
Kalabasfontein farm 116–117
Kgobadi family 31, 32–33, 35
killings 25–26, 33–34, 37–43, 45, 60, 89,
   131–132
   see also dead bodies; death
Kitchener, Lord 17
Klatzow, David 39–40
Koster 71
Kraft, L. 92

L
labour
   bureaus 78–79
   cheap 12, 75, 85–88
   division of 63–66
   prison labour system 5–7, 12, 37,
      40–46, 52, 55, 60–65, 75, 78–82
   recruitment 57, 59, 62–64, 74, 86
   shortage of 12, 52, 54–55, 80, 82–83,
      88–89, 107–108
   tenants 27, 52, 63, 74, 119–120,
      125–127, 129
Lacey, Marian 62–63, 86–87
land
   expropriation without compensation
      21, 34, 125, 137–138
   home and 63, 74–75, 94–96, 116,
      118–119, 121, 133–136
   meaning of 17–22
Land Act of 1913 19, 32, 88, 133–134
land dispossession
   Afrikaners 93–94
   anxiety of white society 52
   colonialism and 125
   history of 31–35
   home and 50
   laws and 91

as material issue 10, 99–100
negative ontological category of Black
   persons 97–98
private property 128
resistance and 131, 134
as spiritual problem 38–39
state and 42–43, 86–88
violence and 18–20, 88, 135
land ownership 16–18, 23
land redistribution 10, 21, 34, 125,
   137–138
Langa, Innocent 90
Langa, Nelson 90
law, farmers as 17, 58–62, 92–95, 121,
   129, 135
Lawrence, H.G. 45–46, 57
laws 9–10, 34, 61, 89–95, 103, 109–112,
   129
Lazarus, Israel 53–54, 86
Lebovo, Phillip 48
Ledwaba, Styles 115–117
Legdaar farm 48, 110, 116, 121–122,
   128–129
Leibrandt, J.R.A. 69
Leslie jail 1–7, *2–3*
Levinas, Emmanuel 8–9, 118, 137
liberals *see* white liberals
livestock *see* cattle
Lotter, Mr 57–58
Lourens, G.S. 69
lynching 92

M
Mabhida, Moses 12
Mafeje, Archie 85
Magwaza, Moses 116, 129–130
Mahlangu, Ngubeza 11, 109–110, 114,
   118, 123, 124
Mahloane, Maria 90
maize 53, 57, 85–87
Malawi *see* Nyasaland, immigrants from
Mamabola, Andrew 91
Mamabola, Violent 91
Mam Winnie 6–7, 9
managers 65–66
Manicheanism 97–98
Marie, Franz 48

Marx, Anthony 94
Marx, Karl 75–76, 99
master-and-servant relationship 21–22
material issues 10, 99–100, 133
Mathebe, Mr 119, 123–124, 129–130
Mating Birds (Nkosi) 77
Mavuso, Mr 126–127
Mayibuye iAfrica slogan 110
Mazibuko, Mr 121–122, 125–129, 136
Mbeki, Govan 113
meat 70
media coverage 12, 45, 55
meeting in Bethal, July 1947 45–47,
    57–58
Meiring, R. 110
memory 120
metaphysics 18, 45, 108
migrants *see* immigrants
mining 85–87, 116
misrecognition 24, 45, 49
Mkhwanazi, Elizabeth 101–102, 104–106,
    109, 113
Mknwena, Jacob 69
Mlotshwa, Leonard 76
'Modern Theory of Colonisation, The'
    (Marx) 76
Mokgoko, Cornelius 48–49, 110, 116
Moloi, Tshepo 11, 27, 101, 119
Moloke, Timothy 37
morality 8, 55, 57
Morgan, Andrew 90
Moses from Alexandra 84–85
Mozambique, immigrants from 52, 63–64
Mpikwa, Elias 71, 73
Mshanelo, Gogo *see* Nkomo, Gogo
    Bongekile Nonhlanhla 'Mshanelo'
Mtembu, Jackson 91
Mtembu, Mary 91
Murray, Martin 57
My Spirit Is Not Banned (Baard) 15

N
Nair, Billy 111
names for farmers 72–73, 119
nationalism 17–18
National Party 78–79, 86, 89
Native Affairs Department 83

Native Commissioner 12, 24, 34, 40, 60,
    81–82, 103
Native Economic Commission (NEC)
    62–63
Native Life in South Africa (Plaatje) 32
'Native Policy for Agriculture' 106–107
native question 14, 77–78
Naudé, Petrus Johannes 51
Ncongwane, Hamilton 103
Ndlovu, Willie 37
NEC *see* Native Economic Commission
negative ontological category of Black
    persons 27, 97–98, 100–102, 104
newspaper reports *see* media coverage
Ngakane, William Barney 4–5, 12, 40–41,
    60, 69–70, 81, 92–93
Nkomo, Gogo Bongekile Nonhlanhla
    'Mshanelo' 35–36, 38–39, 50, 98
Nkosi, Lewis 77
nowhereness *see* ontological nowhereness
Nsibande, Mr 105
Nxumalo, Henry 12–13, 55, 59, 66–74, 76,
    87, 115–118
Nyasaland, immigrants from 52, 54, 61,
    63–64, 120

O
ontological anxiety 94, 126–128, 136
ontological nowhereness
    of children 129–130
    of farmworkers 17, 25, 61, 75, 89, 98,
        122–123, 137
    land dispossession and 19, 29, 32,
        132–134
ontology 18, 131–132
Other 9, 13, 15, 20–21, 49, 118–119,
    136–137
Otherwise, to write 15, 20–21, 118–119

P
PAC *see* Pan Africanist Congress
Pact government 86
Pan Africanist Congress (PAC) 111
pass laws 12, 61–62, 71, 84–85
paternalism 21–23, 35, 43–45, 66, 104,
    106–110, 122–123, 136
peasant wars 112–113

Penal Reform League of South Africa 5, 60, 69–70
petty offenders' scheme 12, 17, 26–27, 34–37, 54–55, 65–66, 78–85, 107
philosophy 18
Phivi (labourer) 4
Picanin (cook) 73
piecework 54
Plaatje, Solomon 19, 31, 32, 133–134
police 68, 81–82, 84, 91–92
political power of Afrikaners 85, 94
poll tax 61, 88
poor whites 86
Population Registration Act 112
Posel, Deborah 12, 79
potato boycott 6, 11–15, *16*, 48–49, 91, 110–111
potatoes that looked like humans 11–14, 19, 33, 66, 95–96, 102, 132, 137, 139
potato farming 4, 25, 52
potato sacks 13, *14*, *16*, 55, 64, 71
Potgieter, P.J. 90
prejudice 33, 45, 136
prison labour system 6–7, 12, 37, 40–46, 52, 55, 60–65, 75, 78–82
  see also petty offenders' scheme
prisons, overcrowding in 12, 75, 82
prisons on farms 14, 65–66, 75, 82–84, 107
private property 16–17, 21–23, 94, 121, 126, 128
Prohibition of Mixed Marriages Act 112
punishment 7–8, 13, 48–49, 62, 65–66, 80, 87

R
race relations 72, 74, 87, 89, 93, 108
racial order 94, 132
racism 75, 89
Rand Daily Mail 57–58, 87, 111
Rand Revolt 86
recruitment 57, 59, 62–64, 74, 86
'Report of Inquiry into the Working Conditions of Prison Farm Labourers' (Ngakane) 69–70
representation 20–21, 45, 49, 107–108
reserves 86–87

Resha, Robert 11–12
resistance
  apartheid state and 109–114
  of farmworkers 80, 84, 137
  negative ontological category of Black persons 100
  political action 49
  violence and 10, 16–17, 75–76, 94–96, 126–128, 135
Rheinallt Jones, Edith 74, 108
Rheinallt Jones, John David 106
Rhodesia, immigrants from 52, 54, 63–64
Rietviel farm 69
rights 23, 29, 61, 89, 91, 112, 127–128
River of Consciousness, The (Sacks) 120
Robert, Margaret 108
rocks 7
Roodebloem farm 117
Rubin, S. 91

S
SAAU *see* South African Agricultural Union
sacks *see* potato sacks
Sacks, Oliver 120
SACTU *see* South African Congress of Trade Unions
Sadika, Dorkus 90
Sadika, James Musa 90
SAIRR *see* South African Institute of Race Relations
Sarah (labour tenant) 117
Sartre, Jean-Paul 95
Schadeberg, Jürgen 62, 115–117
schooling *see* education
Schurvekop farm 116
scorched-earth policy 17, 52
Scott, Reverend Michael 12, 35, 46–48, 54–58, 61, 68, 87, 116–118
'Scramble for Labour is Root Cause' (*The Star*) 83
seasonal workers *see* immigrants
Secretary for Native Affairs 82
Secretary of Justice 82
security of tenure 134
seeing yourself 7
self-image 104–105

servants 32
Shakespeare, William 6–7
Shumbo, Johannes 110
Sibande, Gert 6, 12, 110
Sibhidla-Saphetha, Ntombikayise 36
Sithole, Mr 121
Siz' Abafane Agency 62
Sizwe, No (Neville Alexander) 100
Skosana, Simon 48–49
slavery 21–22, 32, 88, 103
Smith, Linda 9
Snyman, Johan 71
socialisation 104–105
social order 9–10
society 97, 99–104, 109
Soko, Mr 119–120
Sonanzi, Alfred 91
Sonanzi, Esther 91
song 'khona le eBethal siyoghuba
    amazambane' 4
Sonneblom Plaas 117
South African Agricultural Union (SAAU)
    83, 106–107
South African Congress of Trade Unions
    (SACTU) 12, 111
South African Institute of Race Relations
    (SAIRR) 5, 20, 37, 40–41, 69–70,
    82–84, 87–89, 103, 106–108,
    122–123
South African Party 86
South African War see Anglo-Boer War
South Africa's Rule of Violence (Duncan)
    95–96
spirits 13, 73, 76, 95–96, 98, 132, 137–138
spiritual eye 15, 24–25, 33, 35–39, 50, 96,
    116, 132–134
squatters, urban 90
Star, The 83, 111
state
    education 106, 108
    farmers and 35, 45–49, 65, 80–87, 89
    resistance to 109–113, 135–136
    society and 27–28, 99
    violence and 26–27, 40–43, 78–79,
        86–87, 92, 109–110, 134
Steyn, Sydney 119
stigma 71

stock see cattle
suicide 101–102
superintendents 66
superiority 132
Suppression of Communism Act 113
'swart gevaar' 17, 80, 112

T
TAU see Transvaal Agricultural Union
Taylorism 54
terror 1–5, 58, 59, 82, 131, 136–137
theorising from the eye 49–50
Thlome, Jantjie 71
ticket system 53–54, 61
title deeds 121, 125, 137
tot system 70
Transkei, immigrants from 120
Transvaal Agricultural Union (TAU) 83,
    86, 89
Transvaal Farmers' Labour Agency 86
trauma 17, 19, 27, 93–94, 98, 102, 136
trees 18
tribalised 79
tuberculosis 61, 70
Tuje, Casbert 62

U
ukuboniswa 36
umbilical cord 18–19, 138
Union of South Africa, formation of 94
United Nations 112
United States of America (USA) 90, 92, 112
Universal Declaration of Human
    Rights 112
Urban Areas Act 81
USA see United States of America

V
Van der Merwe, Paul J. 69
Van Niekerk, Hermanus 69
Van Riebeeck, Jan 79
Van Wyk, Frederick 40–41, 43–45, 49, 81,
    92–93, 122–123
Verster, V.R. 82–83
violence
    anxiety of white society 50, 77–78,
        89–95, 126–128, 134

education and 27, 98–99, 104–109
on farms 1–9, *2–3*, 25–26,
    45–49, 65–76, 87–88,
    101–104, 118, 135
futurity of 9–10, 73–76, 125–126,
    131–132, 136
killings 25–26, 33–34, 37–43, 45, 60,
    89, 131–132
labour shortage and 54–58, 83
land ownership and 16–23, 135
laws and 10, 34, 62, 91–95
punishment 7–8, 13, 48–49, 62, 65–66,
    80, 87
race relations and 13
resistance and 9, 95–96
slavery and 22
social order and 10
state and 26–27, 40–43, 78–79, 86–87,
    92, 109–110, 134
visions 36, 38, 50
voice of farmworkers 66–68, 72
Vusi (labour tenant) 116

W

wages 53, 61, 65, 70, 89
Way I See It, The (Schadeberg) 62, 117
Webster, Eddie 6, 7
Welsford, V.S. 103
Weston, M.L. 84
white liberals 43–45, 49, 93, 108, 122–123
white society, anxiety of 13–14, 17, 23, 26,
    50, 52, 75–78, 89–99, 112, 126–128,
    131–136
white workers, protection of 86
Wilde, Oscar 97
Wilson, Francis 94
Wooler, B.H. 48
working conditions on farms 35, 69–70,
    89, 106, 114, 122
Wretched of the Earth, The (Fanon) 95

Z

Zaaiwater farm 69
Zimbabwe *see* Rhodesia, immigrants from
Zondagsfontein farm 69